D1255178

BOOKS BY ALBERT C. KNUDSON

THE VALIDITY OF RELIGIOUS EXPERIENCE
THE DOCTRINE OF REDEMPTION
THE DOCTRINE OF GOD
THE PHILOSOPHY OF PERSONALISM
PRESENT TENDENCIES IN RELIGIOUS THOUGHT
THE PROPHETIC MOVEMENT IN ISRAEL
THE RELIGIOUS TEACHING OF THE OLD TESTAMENT
BEACON LIGHTS OF PROPHECY

The Validity of Religious Experience

ALBERT C. KNUDSON
Dean of Boston University School of Theology

The Fondren Lectures

THE ABINGDON PRESS
NEW YORK CINCINNATI CHICAGO

KNUDSON
THE VALIDITY OF RELIGIOUS EXPERIENCE

Printed in the United States of America

To

President Daniel L. Marsh

With warm appreciation of his administrative genius and of his distinguished service to theological education

CONTENTS

PREFACE

SINCE the beginning of the Evangelical Revival two centuries ago religious experience has been a subject of increasing interest. Out of this interest has grown a new emphasis in theology. The apologetic of the Church has become empirical. Experience has become the chief test of religious as well as scientific truth. But along with this pronounced empirical tendency there has arisen much unclearness and confusion of thought with reference to the meaning of religious experience and the basis of its validity. To help clarify thought in this field and to introduce the reader to what I regard as a valid, adequate, and consistent philosophy of religious experience, is the purpose of the present volume.

The chapters of the book were delivered as the Fondren Lectures at the Southern Methodist University in the month of February, 1937. To Dr. Eugene B. Hawk, Dean of the School of Theology, I am deeply indebted for many courtesies shown me during the week spent in Dallas.

My thanks are due Dean Shirley Jackson Case for the privilege of using freely an article on

"The Apologetic Values of Religious Experience" contributed to *The Journal of Religion* for October, 1935.

I wish also to express my gratitude to Dr. James T. Carlyon, Dr. Edgar S. Brightman, and Dr. Earl Marlatt for reading the manuscript and making a number of valuable suggestions.

ALBERT C. KNUDSON.

CHAPTER I

THE NATURE OF RELIGIOUS EXPERIENCE

"Experience" is an ambiguous word; and not only is it ambiguous, it is *multiguous*. It breeds more problems than it solves. Nevertheless, it cannot be dispensed with. There is no adequate substitute for it; and even if there were, we should hardly be able to displace it, so firmly is it embedded in current usage. The best we can hope to do is to bring about greater discrimination in its use; and this we may do by pointing out its various meanings and defining each of them with as great precision as possible. This applies to the word in its reference both to experience in general and to such specific forms of it as religious experience.

Experience and Consciousness

The first thing to be determined in the analysis of experience is its relation to consciousness. Consciousness implies a distinction between subject and object. This distinction need not be metaphysical. The subject may make itself or its own mental states its object. But so far as psychological form is concerned there must be in consciousness, either implicit or explicit, a distinction between subject and object. Consciousness must be a consciousness *of* something *by* someone. And the question we raise is whether this holds true also of experience. The common view is that it does. Experience is necessarily dualistic. It implies both an experient and an object experienced. It is an experience both *of* something and *by* someone. It is in a word synonymous with "experiencing." It means conscious experience. Without consciousness there is no experience in the proper sense of the term.

So it seems to most people. But during the past thirty or forty years an abstract conception of experience has been coming into vogue in certain philosophical circles. The supposed necessary connection of experience with a conscious subject has been severed, and experience has been identified with its objective content or with the total course of events without reference to a subjective experient. A. N. Whitehead, for instance, say that "Consciousness presupposes experience and not experience consciousness."[1] Still more distinctly John Dewey tells us that experience does not mean "experiencing," and has no necessary connection with "conscious-

[1] *Process and Reality,* p. 197. Quoted repeatedly by William Temple in *Nature, Man and God,* pp. 112, 121, 217, 490.

ness." It includes, we are told, "all history on this earth," and by history we are to understand "both objective conditions, forces, events and also the human record and estimate of these events." Indeed, experience "denotes the whole wide universe of fact and dream, of event, act, desire, fancy, and meanings valid and invalid."[2] Thus interpreted it is evident that experience has no distinctive meaning. It is everything. And such a use of the term is manifestly highly confusing. Morris Cohen hardly goes too far when he condemns it as "perhaps the outstanding scandal of recent philosophy."[3]

The question naturally arises in this connection as to how such an impersonal use of the word could have arisen and gained currency. The answer is to be found in the recent history of philosophy and psychology. Three tendencies or developments in particular have contributed to it.

The first is absolute or Hegelian idealism and its continued influence in current thought. According to this type of philosophy the universe as a whole is in its essential nature Thought or Experience. The experience is that of the Absolute; but no sharp distinction is drawn be-

[2] *Experience and Nature,* pp. 8-10.
[3] *Reason and Nature,* p. 453.

tween human and divine experience. The result is that the whole objective world is spoken of as "experience" without distinct reference to a conscious subject. Originally this use of the word "experience" had an idealistic and more or less pantheistic background and would have been regarded as meaningless apart from it. But some thinkers, such as John Dewey, who began as neo-Hegelians and later adopted a naturalistic or realistic position, continued to use the word in its objective and universal sense after they had renounced their idealism; and in so doing they completely detached it from its earlier necessary connection with spirit and consciousness. The result was a purely impersonal use of the term. What led to it was the "naturalizing" of the term by Hegelian converts to philosophical naturalism.

Another cause of the change in the use of the word is the revolt against dualism that has characterized much of Anglo-Saxon philosophy during the present century.[4] This revolt has to some extent been connected with absolute idealism. The absolute idealist sought to overcome the dualism of thought and thing or idea and object by reducing things or objects to thoughts or ideas and merging them all in one compre-

[4] A thorough critical account of this movement is to be found in *The Revolt Against Dualism,* by Arthur O. Lovejoy.

hensive Experience. This type of monism is sometimes called pan-subjectivism. More recently another type of monism has arisen, known as neo-realism and at times referred to as "pan-objectivism." What neo-realism aims to do is to reduce thought to things. Ideas, we are told, are identical with things. There is no separate class of ideas, but only the one class of things, "ideas being the subclass of those things that happen to be known." Things enter the mind, and when they do so become ideas. Ideas, therefore, are simply things in a certain relation, the relation of being known. But by "things" the neo-realist does not understand the substantial things of common sense; he means aggregates of qualities; indeed, he goes beyond that and ascribes a kind of thinghood to "concepts" and "relations." He objectifies what we have been accustomed to regard as subjective elements in experience, and attributes to the "psychological" objects of consciousness a sort of independent metaphysical existence. In this way he has created an intellectual atmosphere favorable to the conception of experience as essentially objective in nature and independent of consciousness.

A third factor that has contributed to what some would regard as the emancipation of "experience" from "consciousness" is the psychological doctrine of the "subconscious" or "unconscious" mind. There is much difference of opinion and confusion of thought as to what is meant or should be meant by the "subconscious" and "unconscious." Some understand by both terms a form of consciousness so that one might, despite the apparent contradiction, speak of a "subconscious" and "unconscious" consciousness. Such a consciousness is supposed to coexist with our ordinary consciousness, and hence it is often spoken of as a *"co-consciousness."* But not a few, such as Freud, take the words "subconscious" and "unconscious" literally and understand them as referring to psychic states or experiences that are wholly devoid of consciousness. What such states or experiences would be like, we do not know, but their existence is, nevertheless, affirmed. And in this way a cleavage is established between experience and consciousness. Experience is thought of as broader than consciousness and inclusive of it, but also as prior to it and in its essential nature independent of it.

The different tendencies in current thought that have led to the impersonal conception of experience are not in and of themselves particularly impressive. A dubious Hegelian usage carried over into an alien naturalistic philosophy, an impossible epistemological monism, and an unintelligible theory of the unconscious mind —such have been its chief sources. But despite its unpropitious origin the conception has acquired considerable vogue. And the result has been the extraordinary laxity and confusion in the use of the word "experience" to which we have referred. Nor has the situation been improved by John Dewey's ingenious contention that "experience for philosophy is method, not distinctive subject matter."[5] It is the method of "denotation," the method of "pointing, finding and showing," and a recognition of the finality and comprehensiveness of this method. Such a conception of "experience" is manifestly artificial and serves no useful purpose. It simply makes confusion worse confounded.

The one way to escape from this confusion is to interpret experience exclusively in terms of consciousness and to restrict the word to conscious experience. If this is not done, the door is opened to all manner of ambiguities and misleading abstractions. Clear and concrete thinking requires us to hold that a strictly impersonal or unconscious experience is a contradiction in terms.

James Ward has pointed out that there are three stages in the history of psychology.[6] In

---

[5] *Experience and Nature,* p. 10.

[6] *Psychological Principles,* pp. 2ff.

the first the fundamental concept was *Life,* in the second *Mind,* and that of the third is *Experience.* The first period was represented by the psychology of Aristotle, which was unduly objective, and the second by the psychology of Descartes, which was unduly subjective. Aristotle laid primary stress on the living organism, its functions and behavior. The soul, it is true, played an important part in his psychology, but he did not arrive at "a clear recognition of what we now call *consciousness* as the central feature of all psychical facts." It was the merit of Descartes that he was the first to make the thinking mind the fundamental and distinctive theme of psychology. By so doing he overcame the hazy materialism and the confusion of psychology with biology which had characterized Aristotelian and scholastic teaching. But he carried the subjective tendency too far. He virtually reduced biology to physics, and thus established a metaphysical dualism of body and mind, that made sense experience inexplicable and that led to a onesided intellectualism. These defects have been, to a considerable extent, overcome in the third period, which has been dominated by the concept of individual experience. In this concept the objective tendency of the Aristotelian psychology and the subjective tendency of the Cartesian psychology are balanced. Individual or concrete experience requires a duality of subject and object. Efforts have been and are being made to revive the Aristotelian standpoint and to eliminate the subject as a necessary element in experience, but the result has been in each instance a false and confusing abstractionism. All concrete experience is owned. It has a conscious subject. It is an experience of something by someone. Recognition of this fact is a precondition of any profitable inquiry into the psychological nature of experience.

Eulogistic Interpretations of Experience

Another fact worth noting is that there are several eulogistic uses of the word "experience."

Etymologically the word connotes expertness, or "the process of becoming expert through experiment." It means skill and efficiency acquired through trial and effort; it means aptitude due to familiarity. It means wisdom or knowledge that is acquired in a practical way and that serves a practical purpose. In this sense of the term experience is of obvious value in all lines of activity. To one who is seeking employment of almost any kind nothing is worth more. It is through experience that we learn how to do things. It is through experience that we gain insight into life and achieve the ability to solve its problems. Experience has thus a unique value, and a certain emotional significance has consequently come to be attached to the word itself.

Another honorific connotation of the term is "sincerity." This appears especially in the religious field. There experience is opposed to formalism, legalism, sacramentalism, intellectualism, social instrumentalism, and every other kind of religious *ism* that places the emphasis elsewhere than on personal experience. Religious experience in this sense stands for inwardness, depth, sincerity, and vitality. It is the form that genuine spiritual religion must take. Experienced religion is the only true religion. Only when religion is translated into feeling and practice does it express its true nature. Without such an inward and vital experience religion is an empty shell. This is emphatically asserted in the prophetic-Christian Scriptures again and again, and has been clearly recognized by the profounder and more earnest spirits in the whole of Christian history. But the Church has often fallen into formalism, legalism, and externalism. Against these evils the Protestant Reformation was a reaction, and since that time, especially since the Wesleyan Revival, there has been a new emphasis on personal religious experience. Experience has come to be regarded as the very essence of religion, as it was not before. Without a vitalized Christian experience there can, according to current evangelical teaching, be no true Christian faith. Experience is the signature of reality in religion as elsewhere. Genuine and sincere religion necessarily expresses itself in experience. Experience thus occupies a place of honor in the field of religion.

A third and still more important honorific connotation of the term is that which has to do with the relation of experience to knowledge or truth. It has in modern times become a common doctrine that experience is the sole avenue to truth. Theory and speculation may have their place in human thought, but they are at the best dubious. Only through experience do we know what truly exists. Through it we have first-hand knowledge. If we have experienced a thing, we are certain of it. Experience and it alone furnishes a valid basis for certainty. If we would establish the truth of any belief, we must appeal to experience. The empirical test is the only adequate test of truth. John Wesley used to speak of experience as "the strongest of all arguments" and as "the most infallible of all proofs."[7] And this is also the common opinion

---

[7] See Umphrey Lee, *John Wesley and Modern Religion,* pp. 136-143; and George C. Cell, *The Rediscovery of John Wesley,* pp. 72-93.

in our day. In the current epistemology experience occupies a unique place of distinction.

Of the three eulogistic uses of the word, which we have briefly described, it is only the last with which we are directly concerned. Experience in the practical sense of expertness and in the religious sense of sincerity has no immediate bearing on the question of the truth of religion. These uses of the term, however, do invest it with an aroma of praise; and this is no doubt one reason why the phrase "religious experience" has become a favorite with many people. It suggests both spiritual worth and a wisdom born of holy living. A vague sense of value thus attaches to the phrase; and this leads many to employ it in an uncritical and often unctuous manner as though the mere pronouncing of the words were sufficient to solve the problems of apologetics and of theology in general.

Such a loose use of the phrase may perhaps have a place in popular discourse; but for critical thought it has, of course, no significance. We here have to do with experience primarily as a source of knowledge. And the question we raise is as to whether a basis for religious belief is to be found in experience. Or, more specifically, does religious experience have apologetic value? Does it have objective validity? and if so, how or why? This is our problem. But before dealing with it we need to define more precisely the nature of religious experience. And to this task the remainder of the present chapter will be devoted.

The Subjective Nature of Religious Experience

In discussing the nature of religious experience there are three main questions that come up for consideration. The first has to do with the subjective or psychological form of religious experience; the second has to do with its objective reference, and the third with its source. We begin with the first.

We have already pointed out that experience must be interpreted in terms of consciousness. If it is not, it loses its distinctive meaning. We may depersonalize the term, as some have done, and apply it to whatever happens to anything, real or imaginary. But in this sense it ceases to be a psychological term. Indeed, it has no definite meaning. It applies to everything, stands in contrast to nothing, and hence means nothing in particular. Its use might as well be discontinued. It has no significance, either philosophical or psychological. If the term is to have a distinct, consistent, and significant meaning, its common and traditional connection with consciousness must be retained. By religious experience we, consequently, understand conscious experience. A strictly unconscious religious experience would be neither "experience" nor "religious."

Unfortunately, the words "unconscious" and "subconscious" have, as we have seen, come to denote certain special types or instances of conscious experience. And hence it has become more or less customary to speak of "unconscious experience," even when the experience referred to is admitted to be conscious. Some, however, have been misled by the phrase "unconscious experience" and have come to think of experience as existing in both a conscious and unconscious state. A distinguished writer on both the psychology and philosophy of religion has, for instance, said that he means by the unconscious "that part of our experience that never comes into our consciousness by any ordinary means," and in another connection he speaks of "inborn or unconscious experience" by way of contrast with "the individual's own consciousness."[8] The idea naturally suggested by such statements as these is that experience exists by itself and may or may not come into consciousness. This may not be what the author actually meant, but his language easily lends

[8] E. S. Waterhouse, *Psychology and Religion*, p. 25, and *The Philosophy of Religious Experience*, p. 157.

itself to this interpretation. In any case such a dual conception of experience has gained currency. There is both conscious and unconscious experience; and of the two the latter is the primary. This dualism is partly the result of the current ambiguous use of the word "unconscious," but it is also due in part to a failure to distinguish between the conditions and effects of experience and the experience itself. What is usually meant by the unconscious or subconscious is the hidden grounds of certain unusual states of consciousness, states that are not occasioned in the ordinary way. These grounds may be hereditary, they may be due to environmental influence, they may be the result of earlier conscious experiences. Indeed, J. B. Pratt says that "the great source of the content of the subconscious is the conscious."[9] But however produced, these grounds or causes of experience should not be confused with experience itself. Experience is to some degree conscious or it is not experience.

Religious experience and the religious consciousness are, therefore, virtually synonymous terms. This means that religious experience is not to be identified with any one aspect of our mental life. It is not merely feeling, merely willing, or merely doing. It embraces all three.

[9] *The Religious Consciousness*, p. 63.

It is necessary to emphasize this fact because there has been a tendency since the time of Schleiermacher to restrict religious experience to a special form of feeling, the feeling, for instance, of absolute dependence. The original motive underlying this conception of religion was commendable. It was a needed reaction against the one-sided intellectualism and moralism of eighteenth-century rationalism. Wesley represented this tendency, and much good resulted from it. But as there are evils in a one-sided intellectualism and a one-sided moralism, so there are evils in a one-sided emotionalism. This became evident in the course of time, and hence there arose a tendency to emphasize the moral and to some extent the intellectual elements in religion. The result has been a better balanced type of religious life. But the old association of religious experience with anti-intellectualism still lingers, and some use the term "experience" to denote the feeling element in the religious consciousness as distinguished from the moral and intellectual elements.[10] The latter have a necessary place in religion, but they are not included in religious experience. Experience is the emotional accompaniment of religious belief and practice, or the emotional

[10] R. H. Thouless, *An Introduction to the Psychology of Religion,* p. 5.

cause or effect of either or both. Wesley had this idea of religious experience in mind when he said of the doctrine of Christian Perfection that "it remains only to *experience* what we believe."[11] The usage is still a common one, but it is out of harmony with the broad meaning usually associated with the word "experience," and implies too limited a conception of religious experience for philosophical and theological purposes.

If religious experience were mere feeling, it would have no apologetic value. It would be a mere fact of consciousness without objective reference. It would witness simply to its own existence, and hence the question of validity could not be raised with reference to it. What gives significance to experience, both religious and sensuous, is its supposed apprehension of an objective reality. Apart from that it would be a meaningless flow of feeling or of impressions. Religious experience we consequently identify with the whole personal religious life, with its beliefs and activities as well as its feelings.

A further point of importance in connection with the nature of religious experience is the fact that all cognitive experience is interpreted experience. There is no such thing as a purely passive apprehension of either the material or

[11] *Journal,* April 3, 1764, Vol. V., p. 56.

spiritual world. In all cognition the mind is active. It is not a mirror passively reflecting an objective order. It is itself a creative process, and only through this creative process does articulate or cognitive experience become possible. It is, therefore, a serious mistake to detach experience from thought or belief and to conceive of it in its purity as an independent entity altogether free from the element of interpretation. This conception of experience is a mere abstraction. There is nothing in reality corresponding to it. All experience is interpreted experience. Kant made that clear once for all so far as sensuous experience is concerned; and its validity as applied to religious experience is equally evident, if not more so. L. P. Jacks has said that "the difficulty about religious experience is not to get it, but to recognize it when it comes."[12] The important as well as the difficult thing is the recognition, and this involves interpretation. Only when the common experience has been properly interpreted does it become truly religious. Interpretation inheres in the very nature of religious experience, as it does in a different way in that of articulate experience in general.

There are some who seem to think that this theory discredits experience as a whole. Their

[12] *Elemental Religion,* p. 53.

minds are haunted by the idea that pure experience is alone to be trusted. Interpretation, they hold, necessarily distorts experience. The result is that some opponents of religion, such as Professor Leuba, naïvely assume that sense experience is immediate and free from subjective interpretation, and then proceed to disprove the validity of religious experience on the ground that it is based on belief and involves interpretive elements. Some religious apologists, on the other hand, are loud in their affirmation that religious experience, like sense experience, is immediate, and that as such it is an independent source and ground of religious belief. Both contentions are unsound. All articulate experience involves interpretation.

The failure to see this has led to much confusion in popular thinking and in particular to a false antithesis between experience, on the one hand, and thought or belief, on the other. It is loosely assumed that experience with and without the qualifying adjective "religious" denotes some sort of independent entity and has some special epistemological or apologetic significance. But just what this entity is or how or why it has such significance is not made clear. This is especially true of religious experience. "It is to be feared," says W. R. Matthews, "that reliance upon religious experience is becoming, in many quarters, a catchword which covers destitution."[13] There is nothing in religious experience that justly exempts it from rational criticism; nor is there any valid ground for treating uncriticized experience as "the final court of appeal in matters of belief." Religious experience as little as any other kind of experience can be accepted at its face value. It must be purged by criticism before its true significance can be brought out. And when this is done, it becomes evident that thought and belief are constitutive factors in it. Experience is no more truly the source of belief than belief is a source of experience. The two go together. We believe what we experience, but we also experience what we believe. As the creative activity of thought is essential to articulate experience in general, so the creative activity of faith is essential to religious experience.

Our conclusion, then, is that from the subjective point of view religious experience, like experience in general, is to be regarded as conscious experience; that it is not to be identified with any one aspect of the mental life; that it involves thinking and doing as well as feeling; and that, like experience in general, it is interpreted experience; it implies the constitutive activity of the human mind. So far as psycho-

[13] *Studies in Christian Philosophy*, p. 6.

logical form or structure is concerned, there is nothing unique or miraculous about it. Religious experience is made up of the common elements of the psychical life and conforms to its general laws. Not even "faith," which in one sense is the characteristic element in religious experience, differs psychologically from faith in general.

The Objective Reference of Religious Experience

For the unique element in religious experience we must turn to its objective reference. The object of religious faith is unique, and because of this fact the human response is such also. The uniqueness of the response, however, does not consist in any novel psychical element or elements but in the general tone or quality of the response. The response is made up of emotional, volitional, and intellectual elements as are other mental states, but the divine object toward which it is directed gives to these elements a distinctive character. It is thus the object of religious experience, and not its psychological constituents, that makes the experience unique.[14]

---

[14] "If we are aware in any way of the presence of the Divine, we are having a religious experience."— Edgar S. Brightman, *The Finding of God,* p. 94.

There is, it is true, some question as to whether religious experience necessarily implies a divine object. An object of some kind it manifestly does have. If conceived as divine, the object may be unreal; but even if unreal, it exercises a determining influence on the experience and is a constituent factor in it. It is, however, claimed that the religious object need not be supernatural or divine. And even if it be regarded as such, its true meaning, we are told, is to be found in the social group. It is society that is the real object of religious faith and devotion. This theory in one form or another has had considerable currency since the time of Auguste Comte. According to it Humanity takes the place of God.

Reference to Deity, we are told, is not essential to religion. The distinctive element in religion is the idea of sacredness. This idea has in the past been conceived superstitiously, and has been attached to a supernatural Object, or Power, or Substance. But this association is not essential to the idea. Sacredness may be conceived naturally, realistically, rationally, ethically; and when this is done, it divorces itself from its earlier supernatural and metaphysical associations and attaches itself to the social ideal and to such social objects as are stamped with the idea of moral obligation. If there is any object truly worthy of reverence, it is human society in its ethical and ideal aspects. Apart from and beyond human society there is nothing that is truly sacred. The sense of sacredness, therefore, which constitutes the heart of religion, is simply "the consciousness of the highest social values."[15] Deity, in the proper sense of the term, has no necessary place in religious experience.

In support of this viewpoint appeal is often made to Buddhism and other atheistic religious movements. But the evidence adduced is far from convincing. These movements, in so far as they are atheistic, may be said to be philosophical rather than religious in character; and in so far as they are truly religious, they imply faith in a more-than-human order. This is distinctly true of original or *Hinayana* Buddhism. It is also a significant fact that when Buddhism became a popular faith, it was transformed into a polytheistic system. In its earlier "atheistic" form it was at least defective as a religion. And this defect consisted, not in the absence of any reference to a superworld, but in the impersonal conception of it. It is here that the fundamental cleavage in religious experience is to be found. All genuine religious experience involves ref-

---

[15] E. S. Ames, *The Psychology of Religious Experience*, p. viii.

erence to a more-than-human Object. But the Object is, in one case, conceived in pantheistic or impersonal terms and, in the other case, in theistic or personal terms. The latter represents the predominant and more characteristic tendency. In it religion comes to its highest and completest fruition. The impersonal tendency is an instance of arrested development. To see in it the norm of religion is to misread the plain indications of history; and still more mistaken is the attempt to find in it a justification of the view that religion requires no reference to a more-than-human order.

To substitute humanity for Deity or social aspiration for the living God is to miss the true genius of religion. It is an effort to get the fruits of religion without religion. Religion cannot be limited to the purely human or social plane without ceasing to be religion. Reference to a divine Object is inherent in the very structure of religion. And no one knows what religion really is who has not at some time or other had within him the consciousness that he must obey God rather than man. Instead of being bound by the social conscience of his day the truly religious man feels himself at times compelled to defy that conscience in the interest of what he regards as a divine command. The social and the religious cannot be completely equated without stifling the religious. Without the belief in a more-than-human Object there would be no distinctive element in religious experience. To separate "the religious" from "religion," as John Dewey [16] seeks to do, and to attribute to the former an existence independent of theistic faith, is to be guilty of an illicit abstraction. An adjectival religiousness may in thought be separated from religion, but not in reality. "Religion" is necessary as the ground and source of the "religious." Only religion can generate the truly "religious."

It is sometimes contended that experiences quite as remarkable as those of religious conversion have resulted from devotion to "social work." This probably has been true in individual cases. But from this one is hardly warranted in concluding that there is nothing distinctive in religious experience and that a purely humanistic preaching would bring about such marvelous moral transformations as have attended the great revivals of religion. Every effort to substitute the moral or social for the religious, or to transform the religious into the moral or social, has thus far failed; and there is every reason to believe that in this respect the future will repeat what has happened in the past. Religious experience will continue, and

[16] *A Common Faith,* pp. 2ff.

it will continue to be what it has been, it will continue to be an experience of God.

In any case it is only such a conception of religious experience that gives any meaning to the inquiry into its validity. If religious experience does not involve faith in the existence of God, it would be absurd to raise the question as to whether it is valid or not. The question of validity can, in the nature of the case, apply to religious experience only in so far as it affirms the objective reality of God. Apart from such an affirmation religious experience would be neither valid nor invalid. It would be simply a psychological fact.

In this connection reference may be made to the view occasionally expressed, that God as an infinite Being cannot be an object of human experience. Human experience is finite and consequently can apprehend only finite objects. As absolute, God lies beyond the reach of experience. This objection comes from two different quarters. It is urged in support of the theory that God is himself a finite Being.[17] It is also urged in the interest of religious agnosticism. In both cases it is based on a mistaken notion of experience and of the elements that enter into it. The assumption underlying it is that experience is a purely receptive process,

[17] Edgar S. Brightman, *The Finding of God*, p. 115.

that external objects somehow enter into it, and that an infinite Being, in the nature of the case, cannot gain access into so limited a receptacle as the human mind. To this assumption the sufficient reply is that experience is the result of a creative activity on the part of the mind, that no object enters the mind either physically or metaphysically, that the mind builds up its own objects on the occasion of external stimuli and in accordance with principles immanent within itself, and that among these principles is an innate capacity to experience and to think the Infinite. Neither thinking nor experiencing is synonymous with imagining. Imagination may require a spatial limitation of its objects, but this does not hold true of thought and experience.

The Source of Religious Experience

The third question relative to the nature of religious experience, above referred to, has to do with its source. We have seen that experience in the proper sense of the term means conscious experience, and we have also seen that religious experience, historically and properly understood, involves reference to a more-than-human Object. We now inquire into the origin or source of religious experience; and here we are confronted with two major questions. One is psychological or historical in character, the other metaphysical or theological.

Neither of these questions admits of a definitive and purely objective solution, and neither of them has a decisive bearing on the validity of religious experience. But it is commonly supposed that they do have such a bearing, and in any case they have figured and still figure so prominently in the discussion of the nature and validity of religion that some account needs to be taken of them.

Those who for one reason or another are unfriendly to the claims of religion usually try to explain its origin by attributing it to some untrustworthy element or elements in human nature, either individual or social. Our fears, for instance, our hopes and desires are, as William James said, "great liars." In some instances they may be safe guides, but for the most part they mislead us. And if it can be shown that religion had its source in one or the other or all of them together, it would by that very fact be to a large extent discredited. Such is the common feeling; and it is for this reason that many people today look upon psychology as "the most dangerous menace to the Christian view of life." They see in the psychological derivations of religious belief a disproof of its validity.[18]

[18] See my *Doctrine of God,* pp. 20ff.

There is, for example, the ancient theory of Lucretius that religion had its source in fear. Fear led men to personify the powers of nature and to seek to placate them. Without such misguided fear there would have been no religion. Then there is the modern theory that religion is due to the objectification of desire or to "wishful thinking." Men wish there was a God and so come to believe there is such a Being. The wish is father to the belief, and hence the belief is untrustworthy.

Essentially the same position is expressed in current psychology by saying that religious belief is due to "suggestion," to "rationalization," and to "projection." Suggestion may take the form either of "auto-suggestion" or "mass-suggestion." That is, the stimulus may come either from the man himself or from the crowd. But in either case the assumption is that the resulting religious experience is wholly subjective and has no valid objective reference. God is simply "the shadow of our subliminal self."

"Rationalization" has been defined as "the production of a reason for, as distinct from the true cause or motive of, an act or conation."[19] It is, we are told, "the outcome of repressed wishes, buried complexes and unresolved con-

[19] A. G. Tansley, *The New Psychology and Its Relation to Life,* p. 160.

flicts in the unconscious."[20] The repressions, complexes, conflicts, and obsessions give rise to false religious and ethical justifications of one's own conduct and the conduct of others. The rationalizing process by which this is brought about may be unavoidable. It may be an inevitable function of the human mind. But the religious and other beliefs to which it leads are nevertheless illusory.

"Projection" is akin to rationalization and equally inevitable as a function of the human mind. It differs from the rationalizing process in that it is concerned with the objectification of desire rather than with its explanation or justification. But in both the mind is supposed to pass from subjective desire to the assumption or affirmation of objective reality; and the process in both instances is unwarranted. Man projects his own self, his hopes, his desires, his ideals upon the external world; and in this way religion originates. God is simply a "projection" of the human mind and has no real existence.

In a similar way it has been argued that religious experience is due to unjust social conditions. Many people live in such a state of abject poverty and utter hopelessness that they turn

---

[20] C. H. Valentine, *Modern Psychology and the Validity of Christian Experience*, p. 20.

away in despair from the real world and gain a measure of contentment by imagining another and better world that awaits them in the future. This was Karl Marx's theory of the origin of religious faith. Religion, he said, "is the striving of the people for an imaginary happiness; it springs from a state of society that requires an illusion, but disappears when the recognition of true happiness and the possibility of its realization penetrates the masses."[21] In other words, economic discontent breeds religious faith and economic content dissipates it. It is wishful thinking, due to unjust social and economic conditions, that gives rise to religious belief, and hence the belief has no rational basis.

Another method of trying to discredit religious experience is to ascribe its origin to prescientific modes of thought. Primitive men explained natural phenomena by referring them to a supernatural Will or wills. But this mode of explanation has been rendered obsolete by science. There is no supernatural Being or beings. Everything is under the reign of natural law. Consequently, there is no valid basis for religious belief. Religion is simply primitive science.

These and similar attempts to destroy the credibility of religious experience by deriving

[21] Quoted by August Bebel, *Woman and Socialism*, pp. 437f.

it from some unworthy psychological or other source have had and still have considerable vogue and influence. But they all rest on unwarranted assumptions. It is, for instance, assumed that if religion can be traced back to crude and superstitious beginnings it is thereby discredited. But by that method all human culture, scientific, ethical, and aesthetic as well as religious, could be discredited. For human life as a whole was crude and superstitious in its beginning. Chemistry had its origin in alchemy, astronomy in astrology, and labor in slavery. But no one regards these facts as inconsistent with the truth of science or the dignity of labor. And so, of course, it should be with religion. Religion no doubt at first manifested itself in crude practices and superstitious beliefs; it was hardly distinguishable from magic and mythology. But this does not mean that it is such today. "No one thinks less of lovely porcelain because it came from common clay, nor is religion stained by the clay of the pit from which it came." The historical origin of a belief or institution does not and cannot decide the question of its present validity and worth. The fact of evolution precludes such an idea. If there is such a thing as human progress, it is obvious that a great historical movement like religion must be judged by its outcome, not by what it came out of. It is its fruits, not its roots, that must be the decisive consideration in our evaluation of it. The contrary notion is a baseless assumption.

Again, it is erroneously assumed that religious experience is discredited by the psychological processes that are at present involved in its production. Not only did it originate in obsolete practices and beliefs; its present existence is due to untrustworthy mental processes. Three of these have been mentioned: suggestion, rationalization, and projection. The fact, however, is that suggestion is a process that enters into human experience as a whole. It sometimes leads to truth and sometimes to error. The latter is usually the case in hypnotism and partisan propaganda; and there are some who limit the term to such illusion-breeding processes. The word thus comes to have for them an unfavorable connotation, and in this sense they apply it to religious experience. But this application of the term is, of course, without justification. It is a begging of the whole question. It is simply an attempt to discredit religious experience by giving it a bad name, and as such is itself an instance of "suggestion" in the narrow and unfavorable sense of the term. In its broader sense suggestion both in the form of autosuggestion and mass-suggestion manifestly plays a part in religious experience as it does in all human experience, but in this sense it does not explain the origin of religion nor in any way prejudice its truth. "Suggestion itself," as E. S. Waterhouse says, "is not sufficient to account for the initiation of religious experience. All suggestion implies an antecedent stimulus from some other source than itself."[22]

This is also true of "rationalization" and "projection." Neither of them originates religious experience and neither of them can discredit it. A brief word of explanation will make this clear. Our human reason is not infallible. At times it goes astray, especially when urged on by some compelling emotion. In such a case as this the reasoning process is called "rationalization." To "rationalize" is to find reasons for what one wants to do or believe. It consists in making subjective desire rather than objective truth the controlling factor in arriving at one's conclusions. This abuse of reason is common in all phases of human life. It appears in religion as elsewhere. But to ascribe the origin of religious faith to it is simply an expression of antireligious prejudice, and is itself an illustration of the "rationalization" attributed to religious believers. The real reason for such a theory of the origin of religious experience is to

[22] *The Philosophy of Religious Experience,* p. 119.

be found in the unbelieving psychologist's hostility or indifference to religion and not in a truly scientific or philosophical study of its nature. The fact is that the "rationalizing" process, which is supposed to give rise to religious experience, could not itself get under way unless there were an already existent religious impulse. The impulse or stimulus must itself come from outside the rationalizing process. Furthermore, it should be noted that the psychological difference between "rationalizing" and sound reasoning is only one of degree. More or less of personal interest underlies both. If absolute disinterestedness were essential to the attainment of truth, truth in its more fundamental and significant sense would be unattainable. No cosmic theory, no philosophy, not even agnosticism, would be possible.

Essentially the same criticism is also to be passed upon the "projection" theory. If God is a projection of the human mind, so also is the world and every object in it. Nothing exists for us except as we think it. It is the objective reference of our thought that alone gives us knowledge of external reality. In this sense we may say that the whole universe is a projection of our minds. And if God is unreal because he is a projection of our thought, so also is the world. It is only on the assumption that projection is at bottom a valid process that we can know anything external to ourselves.

It is thus evident that there is nothing in the historical origin of religious experience, nor in the psychological processes involved in it, that is inconsistent with its essential validity. The basal error in the various theories we have considered is their assumption that the religious element in human experience can be deduced from the nonreligious. This might be possible, if there were nothing unique or distinctive in religion. If the objects of religious faith were the objects of common desire, it might be possible to derive the belief in them from wishful thinking. But religious experience is unique and can be derived only from *religious* desire. Only religion can generate religion. Mere wishful thinking cannot be the source of religion. Only wishful thinking of a religious type can lead to religious belief. Otherwise we would be deriving something from nothing. If desire is the source of religion, it must be not desire in general but *religious* desire. In other words, there must be a native capacity for religion before there can be religious experience. And this native capacity does not, as a matter of fact, consist in mere desire. It involves a sense of "ought." It seeks not merely to gratify a wish, but to fulfill a duty. It recognizes in religion not only a good to be enjoyed but a sanctity to be reverenced and obeyed. It is this that is most characteristic of religion. The true basis of religion is to be found not in a wish philosophy but in an *ought* philosophy. It is faith in an obligatory ideal that lies at the root of religion. And this faith or the capacity for it is inborn. It is "the image of God" within us. It is not an accidental addition to human nature. It is not derived from anything simpler or more elementary. It is structural within the human mind, and as such stands in its own right. It cannot be discredited by any fancied deduction from a nonreligious source, either psychological or sociological.

Parallel to the attempt to overthrow religious faith by deriving it from some unworthy human source is the attempt to justify it by deriving it from a divine source. The latter is the type of apologetic that has prevailed throughout most of the Church's history. It has, however, not been uniform in character. It has conceived religious experience in different ways, and has undergone important developments.

For a long time the redemptive power of God was supposed to enter human life in subconscious form through the sacraments and through membership in the church and submission to its authority. Just how the divine grace was thus mediated to men, we do not know. Its presence in them did not as a rule emerge in consciousness. It was supposed to operate in them as a mysterious essence, divinizing their nature, transforming what was mortal in them into the immortal, effecting the forgiveness of their sins, and thus through a quasi-metaphysical or legalistic process preparing them for eternal fellowship with God. At times it might, as with the mystics, take the form of conscious experience. But this was not its essential nature. The divine grace was, rather, a subconscious substance or process, in whose reality the recipient might believe but whose reality did not consist in conscious belief.

At the Reformation a significant change took place. Participation in the divine grace now came to be regarded as conditioned by faith, not by any purely external act or relationship; and faith was looked upon as a conscious act. But unfortunately faith gradually acquired a double meaning. It denoted a conscious experience, but it also came to denote a divine act within us. And under the exigencies of theological debate the latter meaning tended to overshadow the former, and, indeed, to be divorced from it. The conscious experience of faith or assurance might be due to a divine act, but it might not. It might have a purely human or natural cause and thus be misleading. This has often occurred in popular revivals of religion, and hence such experiences are open to serious question. They do not necessarily indicate the actual presence of the Divine Spirit. And, on the other hand, a divine act of faith within us does not necessarily result in a corresponding mental state. A man may have saving faith and not know it, just as he may think he has it and be mistaken. In other words, psychological faith and metaphysical or actual faith do not necessarily go together.

The divorce thus established between faith as a conscious experience and faith as a mysterious and inscrutable divine act was, on the whole, unfortunate. It led early in the eighteenth century to a marked decline of religious interest in England. Spirituality sank to a low ebb. It was to meet this situation and to make religion once more a vital power that Wesley began to proclaim the possibility of "a feeling-possession of God," the possibility of a conscious assurance of the divine grace. The new message met with an extraordinary response, a response so remarkable that since his time evangelical Christianity in the Anglo-Saxon world has been largely dominated by it. Almost everywhere in England and America stress has been laid on vital religious experience, and it has been generally assumed that such an experience points directly to a divine source. The divine act and the human experience go together. One implies the other. This has come to be the common belief. Of late, however, a revival of the older Calvinistic distinction between experience and faith has taken place. The tendency at present with Karl Barth and his followers is to ascribe "religious experience" to man and "faith" to God. Emil Brunner, indeed, goes so far as to say that *"believing* God is the antithesis of *experiencing* God. Our faith stands opposed to all experience just as it stands opposed to death and the devil."[23] This supposed antithesis of experience and faith is grounded in the Barthian assumption that there is "an endless qualitative difference between time and eternity," that is, between man and God, and that no *human* experience can in the nature of the case lay hold of God. A real apprehension of God can come only through a divinely produced faith. Such a faith, it is true, may lead to a corresponding experience, but the experience in that case is no longer "experience" in the ordinary human sense of the term. It is due to the Divine Spirit and hence is better described as "faith." If it be called a religious experience, it must be distinguished as "genuine" religious

---

[23] *Die Mystik und das Wort,* p. 188.

experience. All religious experience that is not divinely produced is illusory. The only valid religious experience is that which is more accurately designated "faith," and its validity is absolutely guaranteed by the fact that it is "the gift of God." It is the source of religious experience, therefore, that is the most significant question in connection with it. If its source be human, it is illusory and untrustworthy. If its source be divine, it is genuine and valid. In a divinely produced faith or religious experience we have the one and only impregnable basis of religious certainty.

This line of reasoning recalls the older doctrine of infallibility and from a purely abstract point of view may have a certain plausibility. But there are two decisive objections to it. In the first place, there is no way of determining with certainty when faith is divinely produced within us. "We can," as Barth puts it, "only believe that we believe." But if this be true, it is obvious that we can never know whether we have true faith or not. We may believe that we have it, but the belief is human and hence can yield no certainty. A divinely produced faith would no doubt be trustworthy, but unless we know that we possess it, it can in the nature of the case be of very little value to us.

In the next place there is no valid ground for

such a sharp distinction between the human and the divine as is drawn by the Barthian theology. No one can determine with certainty where the human ends and the divine begins. The two overlap, and only in a general way can they be distinguished from each other. To ascribe experience to man and faith to God is to draw an arbitrary distinction. Religious experience and faith are virtually synonymous terms. There is no truly religious experience without faith, and there is no vital faith that is not experienced. A faith that exists simply as a mysterious and inscrutable act of the Divine Spirit is an empty abstraction. The only value that such a conception of faith has is that it directs attention to the fact that true religious experience necessarily implies an immanent divine activity. Experience of this kind is not merely a human quest after God, it is a divine quest after man. It is not simply the outreaching of the human spirit, it is the indwelling of the Divine Spirit. But the divine indwelling does not exclude human co-operation. Nor is anything gained by deriving religious experience exclusively from a divine source. If man is made in the image of God, there is no reason why his mental processes should not be fundamentally trustworthy, especially when they are guided by the Divine Spirit. And if it be maintained that a purely divine thought activity would be more trustworthy, nothing would be gained by such a contention, since the divine activity could only manifest itself through a concurrent human activity. The quest after an absolute objective certainty is thus doomed to failure. In genuine religious experience the human and the divine intermingle, and there is no way of eliminating the human factor without eliminating man himself. It is important to recognize with Barth that true faith or religious experience implies the presence of God, but it is also important to recognize that it implies likewise the concurrent activity of man. It is a divine-human rather than an exclusively divine source to which we must trace our religious experience.

It may also be added that in emphasizing the divine immanence in religious experience it is important that we distinguish between the "supernatural" and the "miraculous." The supernatural, properly understood, is not the antithesis of the natural, as is the miraculous. An experience may be "natural" from one point of view and at the same time "supernatural" from another point of view. It may be natural in the sense that it conforms to the laws of psychology, and at the same time it may be divine in its causation or ultimate source, and in this sense supernatural. This is true of all nonvolitional experiences. But it is true in a special sense of religious experiences. For the latter carry with them a more or less distinct consciousness of their divine source. In this respect they have a "supernatural" reference and a "supernatural" content. But they are not on that account psychological miracles. If they were, there could be no psychology of religion. Such a science presupposes a large degree of regularity and uniformity in the religious life. There may be and probably are what may properly be called psychological miracles of a religious character. But miracle does not inhere in the nature of religious experience. When we refer conversion, providential care, "guidance," moral inspiration, love, peace, and joy to the Divine Spirit, we do not or ought not to mean that they are "miraculous" in nature. For the most part they conform to law. Psychological law no more excludes divine agency than does cosmic law.

This fact has often been overlooked. The result is that many have tried to find a basis for the validity of religious experience in the theory that such experiences as the new birth cannot be psychologically explained and hence must be referred to a divine cause; while others, such as J. H. Leuba,[24] have argued that all religious experiences are psychologically explicable, and

[24] *A Psychological Study of Religion,* pp. 207-277.

hence are illusory in so far as they contain a reference to a transcendent Being. These two antithetical types of thought are both the outcome of a false naturalism. They assume that if there be a God, he can manifest himself in experience only through a psychological miracle. If a religious experience is a miracle, it has apologetic significance, otherwise not. This assumption misconceives the relation of God to the natural order, and has no valid basis. If adopted, it would in scientific circles justly be regarded as a surrender to unbelief.

Miracle is not, and cannot, be made the basis of a sound empirical apologetic. The actual grounds of such an apologetic are quite different. What they are and to what extent they are valid will be the theme of the succeeding chapters.

CHAPTER II

IMMEDIACY AND TRUTH

Religious experience is conscious and cognitive. Through it we profess to "know" God, and to know him as a living God, a God active in human life. But how do we know him? Or, rather, what valid basis, if any, does our "knowledge" have? To this question there are in the main three answers. One emphasizes the *immediacy* of religious experience, another emphasizes the *value* of religious experience, and the third lays stress on the principle of *self-verification.* To each of these a chapter will be devoted. We begin with the first, the immediacy of religious experience as a ground for believing in its truth.

The Scientific and Philosophical Criticism of Experience

Experience has in modern times the distinction of being regarded as the chief, if not the sole, source of knowledge, and hence there is a certain prejudice in favor of any belief that professes to be based upon it. But this prejudice does not logically carry us very far. For it is obvious that there are various kinds of experience, and that some experiences may be regarded as objectively valid, while others are manifestly not such. Furthermore, it has become increasingly clear that no experience is a pure transcript of objective reality, and that the tendency of critical thought has been to limit more and more the range of the objective validity of experience.

Take, for instance, sense experience. It is interesting and instructive to note the different ways in which the extent of its objective validity has been curtailed by the advance of science. In the ancient world it was discovered that things are not as they seem and that a distinction must be drawn between what we call primary and secondary qualities. "Only in opinion," said Democritus, "consists sweetness, bitterness, warmth, cold, color; in truth, there is nothing but atoms and empty space."[1] In this statement a very significant limitation was placed upon the cognitive trustworthiness of sense experience. The secondary qualities seem objective. They are given as such in experience. But in reality they are subjective. Only the primary or spatial qualities are truly objective.

A second significant narrowing of the validity of sense experience is represented by the Copernican astronomy. In it the common-sense view of the heavens was flouted. Even men of science

[1] Quoted in F. A. Lange's *History of Materialism,* I, p. 23.

were at first scandalized by it. "The eyes are witnesses," said Melanchthon in a work on physics published six years after the death of Copernicus, "that the heavens revolve in the space of twenty-four hours. But certain men, either from love of novelty, or to make a display of ingenuity, have concluded that the earth moves; and they maintain that neither the eighth sphere nor the sun revolves. Now, it is want of honesty and decency to assert such notions publicly, and the example is pernicious."[2] That so distinguished a scholar as Melanchthon should have expressed himself in such terms as these may at first seem strange, but it is not surprising when one takes into account the thought of his day. The new astronomical theory did as a matter of fact contradict the most obvious and overwhelming testimony of the senses. The universe of sense experience is a geocentric universe and always will remain such. To doubt its objective existence must at first have seemed to people generally utterly absurd. Yet the Copernican astronomy in the course of time triumphed, and the authority of sense experience was correspondingly curtailed.

A third curtailment is at present being brought about by the new electronic theory of

---

[2] Quoted by A. D. White in *A History of the Warfare of Science with Theology,* I, pp. 126f.

matter. Matter seems to our senses to be extended substance; and this is the view of it implied in the older atomic theory. Atoms were supposed to be homogeneous and indivisible, but today we are being told that they are made up of protons and electrons and that they are "as porous as the solar system." If all the unfilled space within them were eliminated and all the protons and electrons of a man's body were collected into one mass, it is said that "the man would be reduced to a speck just visible with a magnifying glass."[3] This is manifestly a revolutionary theory. It practically eliminates the common lumpish conception of matter and puts in its place an unpicturable and dynamic conception, thus making a still further serious encroachment upon the validity of sense experience.

Along with these scientific criticisms of sense experience there has gone an even more drastic philosophic criticism; the upshot of which is that sense experience is purely phenomenal, that it yields no direct metaphysical insight, and that it is valid only in the sense that it apprehends an objective order common to us all. What the cause of this order is, we do not know. So far as sense experience is concerned, it may be either a blind energy or a personal Being.

[3] A. S. Eddington, *The Nature of the Physical World,* p. 2.

But some agency, either personal or impersonal, our rational nature requires us to affirm. It is, furthermore, implied in sense experience that there is a metaphysical distinction between the conscious subject and the objective order apprehended. This dualism is inescapable, so far as human thought and experience are concerned. The various attempts made to avoid or overcome it during the present century have failed. They have all been purely verbal monisms.[4] There is no way of identifying thought with thing or idea with object without falling into self-contradiction and absurdity.

It is also impossible to bring thought into such immediacy of contact with things that our knowledge of them is absolutely indubitable. In saying this I am not thinking of the incommensurability of mind and matter. I am thinking of the physiological and physical conditions of cognition. We arrive at a knowledge of the external world through the nervous system and through various objective media. These physical and physiological media preclude the possibility of absolute immediacy in the knowledge of sense objects. All knowledge of the objective order is necessarily mediated. There is nothing in sense experience as such that guarantees its validity. There is in it, it is true, a sense of

[4] See *The Revolt Against Dualism,* by Arthur O. Lovejoy.

givenness, but this sense is often vague and misleading.

As further evidence that there can be no absolute immediacy in sense experience it has been shown that the mind in knowing is not passive. It does not passively receive a ready-made knowledge. It does not passively mirror objective reality. It is itself creative. It builds up its own world in response to external stimuli. Nothing is carried bodily into the mind. The mind shapes and fashions its own objects. Nothing can exist for the mind except as the mind thinks it. Thinking is a mental activity and can be nothing else; and as such it is a mediating factor in all cognitive experience. There is no way of escaping it. The mental equation cannot be eliminated from human knowledge. Only through the mediation of thought can reality be apprehended. This truth was made clear once for all by Immanuel Kant.

Psychological and Metaphysical Immediacy

The foregoing conclusions drawn from the philosophical and scientific criticism of sense experience have manifestly an important bearing on religious experience, and should be borne in mind as we now proceed to a discussion of the immediacy of the latter and its cognitive significance. Religious experience differs from sense experience in that it has a different object. It presupposes the objects of sense experience and may include them; but in so far as it is religious, it goes beyond them. It implies a reference to a more-than-human and a more-than-cosmic Object. This reference is "immediate" in the same way that the objective reference of sense experience is. That is, it is given in and with the religious experience itself and forms an integral part of it. It is not a conscious addition to or deduction from the experience, but an ultimate and essential constituent of it. The experience would not be religious without it. Religious experience involves an immediate conscious reference to a Divine Being.

But this conscious reference takes different psychological forms. It may take the form of faith or trust. Luther, for instance, in *The Greater Catechism,* asks "what it means to have a God or what is God," and then answers by saying that "God is one from whom we expect all good, and in whom we can take refuge in all our needs, so that to have a God is nothing else than to trust and believe in him with all our hearts."[5] This is in line with the later Kantian teaching that God is not a Being whom we perceptually apprehend. He is, rather, a Being

[5] *Luther's Primary Works,* edited by Wace and Buckham, p. 34.

whose existence we postulate. We may act as if he existed, we may "bet our lives that there is a God," and in this way enter into a vital experience of him. But the experience is an act of faith rather than an act of perception. It is something generated within us rather than forced upon us from without. It grows out of the demands of our moral and spiritual nature rather than out of the compulsion of events. It has its source in belief rather than in the sensibility. But it contains nevertheless an immediate reference to a Divine Object; and the immediacy of this reference carries with it a conviction of reality. The basis of this conviction, however, is fiducial rather than perceptual or logical.

Another form that the objective reference of religious experience takes may be described as the causal or logical. Many religious experiences, especially those associated with conversion, seem to come from without and to be due to a higher power. Professor Reinhold Seeberg, of the University of Berlin, in speaking of a profound religious experience of his own said: "I did not bring this about myself, and no man was the cause of it. The will of God in his omnipotence penetrated into my heart."[6] "We feel

[6] Quoted by J. H. Leuba in *A Psychological Study of Religion,* p. 228.

within us," says a French Protestant, "a being that is not ourselves; we see born within us new ideas, perceptions, real revelations that do not come from ourselves."[7] This is a common characteristic of sudden, unexpected, and vivid religious experiences, and may be said to be implicit in all religious experience. The experient feels himself under external control and spontaneously attributes his experiences to a divine source. It was so with Paul (2 Corinthians 12. 1-4) and has been such with multitudes of others. To experience conversion and any kind of religious ecstasy is to feel that a higher power has invaded one's being and wrought a change within one. This is a fact attested by the whole of Christian history. We refer our religious experiences, especially those of an unusual character, to the Divine Spirit, and we do it so instinctively that we are not aware of the process. It seems to be an immediate apprehension on our part of a divine agency within us. As a material object seems to be the cause of its own perception, so it is with the things of the spirit. Spiritual perception seems to be begotten of the Spirit. So instantaneous is the process by which this conclusion is reached that it does not seem to be an inference. It seems to be part of the original religious perception or experience. But

[7] Quoted by J. H. Leuba, *ibid.,* p. 222.

whatever be the precise nature of the objective reference, the reference itself is causal or logical in character. It springs from a religious experience so sudden or so vivid that it seems to bear in itself the mark of a transhuman origin.

The third psychological form assumed by the objective reference of religious experience is the mystical sense of presence. This type of religious experience is to some extent involved in the other two, but in conjunction with them it is subordinated, in the one case, to faith, and in the other, to the idea of cause. Here the sense of presence is immediate. It is "a sense of present reality more diffused and general than that which our special senses yield," but nevertheless "as definite and convincing as sight or touch could make it." It is a perception, "a perception of a reality existing independently of us," "a perception of something there," "a feeling of objective presence," "a Witness of God in the soul." Mystics have described in manifold ways their consciousness of the Divine Presence; but however varied their descriptions of it may have been, they have usually been agreed on its essential characteristics. They have emphasized (1) its immediacy, (2) its certainty, and (3) its sense of union with Deity, both ethical and metaphysical.

These three qualities stand closely related to

each other. The immediacy of religious experience gives rise to the feeling of certainty, and the feeling of certainty is grounded in the theory of union with God. A brief exposition will make this clear.

Immediacy may be either psychological or metaphysical. It is in the former sense that the term is usually applied to experience. Sense experience seems to reflect or lay hold of its object without any intervening agency. And so also does religious experience. The latter is "more like a sensation than an intellectual operation properly so called." Indeed, William James goes further and declares that it is "absolutely sensational in its epistemological quality."[8] We have in it an immediate face-to-face presentation of what seems to be real. There is in it no conscious intervention of thought, no mental process that dims the distinctness with which the Divine Presence is apprehended.

The result is that the mystical experience carries with it "an absolute assurance of the reality of the Divine." It is so "immediate," so "convincing," so "irresistible" that it seems to be a divine revelation rather than a human experience. God is so immediately revealed in it that the experient has no doubt as to his existence. "God," he says, "is more real to me than

[8] *The Varieties of Religious Experience,* pp. 64, 424.

any thought or thing or person." And this experience, he insists, is "unassailable" and "invulnerable."

But on what rational ground can this claim be made? The psychological immediacy of mystical experience certainly does not warrant it. We have such immediacy in sense experience, and it is there often misleading. So long as there is in our experience a dualism of idea and object or of thought and thing there can obviously be no absolute immediacy and no absolute certainty. Immediacy from the dualistic standpoint is necessarily relative. There may in any act of cognition be a parallax between idea and object. Error is always possible. The only way that this possibility could be avoided, would be by a metaphysical union between subject and object or between thought and thing. But this is manifestly impossible on the sense plane despite all the labored attempts of neo-realists and absolute idealists. Epistemological monism contradicts the patent facts of sense experience.

The relation of the soul to God, however, is different, we are told, from its relation to the external world. In the latter case there is a necessary otherness. Complete union is impossible. Hence, in our experience or knowledge of finite objects, personal or impersonal, there is an ineradicable dualism. But in our relation to the Infinite the situation is different. Here complete union is possible. Hence, in our experience and knowledge of God there may be absolute immediacy and indubitable certainty. Some mystics, for instance, tell us that the self may become so identified with God as to know God with the same immediacy that it knows itself. "The eye with which I see God," said Meister Eckhart, "is the same eye with which he sees me." Only on this assumption, he held, can we really know God. "I must be completely he and he I; so that this he and this I become and are one." The union here affirmed as possible between the soul and God is manifestly not merely psychological, a union of feeling, nor merely ethical, a union of will. It is a real metaphysical union. And in such a union, if it were actually realized, there would, we shall have to admit, be a valid basis for the absolute immediacy and certainty that the mystics have claimed for their experience of God. In this respect they are, as Royce said, the only true or thoroughgoing empiricists.

But such a union with Deity as Meister Eckhart affirmed is inconceivable. Even the mystics would admit that. And not only is it inconceivable, it is self-contradictory. For what seems to be meant by it is that the finite self is so merged with Deity as to lose its own self-identity. And under those circumstances it would be absurd to talk about its knowing God. If the self has ceased to exist as an independent and self-conscious being, any knowledge on its part would be out of the question. The union with God, which was supposed to guarantee the validity of the mystical experience or knowledge of God, thus cancels the possibility of such an experience or knowledge. Nor does it help matters to be told that the soul in some inconceivable way maintains its identity despite its complete metaphysical oneness with God. For this is simply to talk nonsense. A certain degree of separation between man and God is essential if there is to be any true knowledge of God on man's part. Absolute union with God does, it is true, make theoretically possible an absolutely immediate experience of him, but at the same time it excludes that independence of man without which there can be no properly human experience or even human existence. Mutual otherness is an indispensable condition of man's experience and knowledge of God. Epistemological monism is as impossible here as in any other form of objective experience.

A rather curious attempt has been made by some to escape the foregoing conclusion. Solovyof, for instance, says that "the reality of the

Deity is not a deduction from religious experience, but the content of it—that which is experienced. If the immediate reality of the higher principle be taken away there would be nothing left of religious experience. It would no longer exist. But it does exist, and therefore that which is given and experienced in it exists also. God is in us, therefore he is."[9] In this argument it is obvious that the author confuses the "noetic quality" of religious experience with a sort of metaphysical conception of the experience. From the cognitive standpoint religious experience refers to a Divine Object and may metaphorically be said to embrace it. But the objective reference or process of embracing may be illusory. There may be no Divine Object actually apprehended in religious experience; and yet the experience would be truly religious so long as the apparent apprehension of Deity forms a part of it. All that is essential to religious experience is faith in God. That he actually exists is no necessary part of the experience. To define religious experience in such a way as to include in it not the idea of God but God himself, as Solovyof seems to do, is to transform it into a kind of metaphysical entity. Only on the basis of some such untenable conception as this could the actual existence of God be in-

[9] *Justification of the Good,* Eng. trans., p. 164.

volved in religious experience. Religious experience cannot guarantee the reality of God so long as it remains experience. All objective experience may be either valid or invalid; and no redefinition or hypostatizing of experience, religious or nonreligious, can alter this fact. Solovyof seems to think that religious experience must be valid in order to be truly religious. But in that case it certainly is open to question whether there is such a thing as truly religious experience. We cannot settle the matter by simply saying that it "does exist." The mere possibility of its existence can be established only by first establishing the existence of God. If there is a God, there may be truly religious experience; if not, there manifestly is no such experience. What we call religious experience has no necessary ontological significance. It may be valid, but it may also be invalid.

Perception, Intuition, and Inference

There is no way, then, by which religious experience may be made an infallible revelation of Deity. There is no way by which the mind may be brought into such immediate contact with external reality that the possibility of error is excluded. Nothing exists for us except as we think it; and our thinking is fallible. It may lead us astray. There is no way of avoiding this possibility. It applies to all our thinking, whether it take the form of sense experience and deductions from it or the form of religious experience and deductions from it.

The mystical claim to absolute immediacy and inerrancy has thus no valid basis.[10] But while this is so, and while no form of objective experience is infallible, it still is true that we do distinguish between what William James called "acquaintance with" and "knowledge about" and what Bertrand Russell calls "knowledge by acquaintance" and "knowledge by description." The distinction is an important one. "Acquaintance with" denotes the knowledge we acquire through direct experience, through sensation and perception. "Knowledge about" is the knowledge we arrive at through description or through inference. The chief difference between the two is that one is direct and the other indirect. Inferential knowledge is indirect or mediate. Perceptual knowledge is commonly spoken of as "immediate." Its immediacy, however, is relative, not absolute. But though relative, it is not devoid of significance. It carries with it a sense of assurance and conviction of reality that the mediacy of inferential knowledge

[10] "There is no immediacy," says Professor Brightman, "in which certainty can be found." See his admirable article on "Immediacy" in *Jahrbuch für die Idealistische Philosophie,"* Bd. I, pp. 87-101.

lacks or possesses in a less pronounced degree. Hence there has naturally arisen among apologists a feeling that it would help the cause of religious faith if it could be shown that religious experience has the same immediacy as sense experience, and that it is sensational or perceptual in its basis rather than inferential. The result has been that considerable effort has of late been made to establish a perceptual or intuitional theory of religious knowledge.

The most significant attempt made in this direction is that by Rudolf Otto, in his well-known book entitled *The Idea of the Holy*.[11] We shall deal with it at some length, but before doing so there are several terms such as "immediacy," "perception," "intuition," and "inference" that call for brief comment.

The word "immediacy" has already been discussed, and little need here be added to what has been said. As applied to perceptions and intuitions it is, of course, not a spatial or metaphysical term. It does not mean that the mind in some mysterious way wraps itself about its objects or enters into such direct contact with them that no mediating agency or instrument of any kind is needed. The term is temporal

---

[11] Characterized by Kenneth Edward as "at once the most significant and the most provocative work on religion which has appeared in our generation." *Religious Experience: Its Nature and Truth*, p. 56.

rather than spatial. It denotes instantaneousness. It means that the mind in its perceptual and intuitional experience goes directly to its objects and does so with such lightninglike rapidity that the act seems to be simple, unitary, undivided. If there are any processes or stages of development in it, they are hidden from view; they do not emerge in consciousness. All that consciousness gives us is the simple, direct, and instantaneous apprehension of the object. And this is what immediacy means as applied both to sense experience and to mystical experience. It does not deny mediation, nor does it deny inference or mental activity of any other kind. What it denies is conscious mediation or inference that proceeds so slowly that the mind is aware of it. Such mediation and such inference form no part of the perceptual act. The act is immediate so far as our consciousness is concerned. But the immediacy is apparent, not real. It is psychological, not metaphysical.

"Perception" in the older psychology was often treated as a simple, original, and unanalyzable form of mental activity. But this view is now obsolete. All perception is recognized to be "acquired perception." We perceive the external world only through the co-operation of the other forms of mental activity. "Will enters in the form of attention. Thought contributes its categories and the sensibility furnishes the raw material. Even reproduction plays an important part."[12] Perception is, therefore, no passive mirroring of objective reality. It is a complex, creative, and transforming process. So much so is this the case that in a sense we are justified in saying with Lotze that "the whole of our apprehension of the world is one great and prolonged deception."[13] The world in its purely objective existence is emphatically not the world that it seems to be in sense perception.

To meet this situation it has been customary to distinguish between phenomenal and metaphysical reality. By phenomenal reality is meant the world of sense experience. This world, despite the subjective and deceptive elements in it, is still a real world, a world common to our finite minds. We do not arbitrarily create it, we find it; and in this sense it is objective. But it becomes such to us only through perception. In perception the mind rationalizes the raw material of sensation, gives to it an objective form, and thus reaches the world of things. It is in this act of projection and in the accompanying consciousness or awareness of external objects that the essence of perception consists.

---

[12] B. P. Bowne, *Introduction to Psychological Theory*, p. 253.

[13] Quoted by G. T. Ladd, *Outlines of Descriptive Psychology*, p. 218.

Perception, however, is not necessarily limited to the physical plane. There is, as we have seen, something akin to it in the mystical sense of presence. And from the speculative standpoint there is no reason why we should regard this sense of presence as illusory. The senses are not the measure of reality, nor is there any adequate ground for holding that the range of perception is the same for all. "There might," as Bowne says, "be a spiritual awareness of reality beyond sense which should be a revelation that could never be judged or tested by sense."[14] And the condition of this perception might be subjective rather than objective. It might be found in the spiritual attitude of the percipient rather than in any unique external stimuli. In any case it is the immediate and elementary conviction of reality which accompanies perception that constitutes its "gist and test," and this conviction manifestly has a place in religious experience. It would, then, seem clear that we are justified in speaking of religious perception as well as of sense perception.[15]

Some, however, prefer the word "intuition"

[14] *The Immanence of God,* p. 75.

[15] F. L. Strickland seems to hold that mystical experiences are not "in any way perceptive." But it would seem to be the word rather than the idea that he rejects. For he says that "in some way the whole of the conscious self, under certain conditions, may respond to supersensory influences." *The Psychology of Religious Experience,* p. 267.

to the word "perception" in speaking of the "noetic quality" or cognitive side of religious experience. This is due in part to the influence of Bergson and in part to the fact that the word "intuition" is not so closely associated with sense experience as is the word "perception." According to Bergson, intuition is a profound and significant phase of human thinking. It is direct and immediate, as is sense perception. But it differs from the latter in several important respects.

For one thing it is primarily concerned with the metaphysical rather than the phenomenal. It has to do with reality rather than with appearance. It is "the metaphysical investigation of what is essential and unique in the object."[16] It is placing oneself by means of intellectual sympathy "within an object" in order to apprehend what is distinctive and "inexpressible" in its nature. It is thus deeper and more penetrating in its insight than sense perception. The latter reflects the exterior rather than the interior of objects.

From this it follows that intuition is a more distinctly spiritual act than sense perception. It is not so largely based upon or conditioned by external stimuli. It is a more completely inward act. It is a kind of "intellectual sympathy," and

[16] Henri Bergson, *An Introduction to Metaphysics*, p. 18.

in its primary and original form manifests itself as self-consciousness. This consciousness "introduces us to the interior of a reality, on the model of which we must represent other realities."[17] Other realities are then akin to the self; and to intuit them is akin to the "intuition of the self by the self." In both instances it is a case of "intellectual sympathy," and in both we have a form of immediacy. "There is," says Bergson, "a reality that is external and yet given immediately to the mind." But this immediacy is not the same as the immediacy of self-intuition. "Sympathy" with other beings can never be wholly the same as sympathy with oneself. There may be kinship between them but never complete identity.

Intuition is said to be "a simple act." It is distinguished sharply from the analyzing and generalizing activity of the mind through which the concepts of science and philosophy are formed. These concepts, we are told, distort reality by concealing its mobile character. In order to reach intuition one must transcend concepts; and one must also transcend sense experience. But this does not necessarily mean that intuition is altogether unique and simple. The very conditions under which it arises point to its being related to life or experience as a whole.

[17] Henri Bergson, *ibid.*, p. 65.

There is, furthermore, no reason why it should not be regarded as a product of the creative activity of thought. Indeed, no other explanation of its articulate character and noetic quality can be given. Pure simplicity would contribute nothing of significance to it.

Bergson distinguishes sharply between "static" religion, the religion of "closed" society, and "dynamic" religion, the religion of "open" society. To the latter he ascribes mystical intuition. These two religions, we are told, differ from each other, not in degree, but in kind. They are opposite to each other. There is no passing from the static to the dynamic "by a mere process of enlargement or improvement." Dynamic or mystical religion emerges as something new, and in its purity is limited to a comparatively small number. It is the experience of a privileged few, and it is such because it is the result of a new and special endowment. It is not simply "a more fervent faith." It does not consist merely in going over the letter of the dogma and retracing it "in characters of flame." It possesses "an original content, drawn straight from the very wellspring of religion." It is a new disclosure of reality to the human spirit, and as such marks a new stage in the history both of religion and of philosophy. This conception of mystical intuition, Bergson argues, is in harmony with his own fundamental doctrine of the *élan vital* or vital impetus.[18]

"Inference" is commonly regarded as a mental process quite distinct from perception and intuition. The latter are direct modes of apprehension, the former indirect. We infer the existence of atoms, of electrons and protons, of ether, and of numerous other objects of scientific and philosophic theory, of which we have no direct experience. We also learn from others of various objects and events that have not come under our own observation. In this way we build up our knowledge about the world. It is all based in one way or another upon inference. This is commonly supposed to be the chief difference between "knowledge about" and "acquaintance with" an object. The latter is direct. It takes the form of perception or intuition; and both of these, it is assumed, exclude inference. They are immediate apprehensions of reality.

This, however, as we have pointed out, is an erroneous assumption. There may be no conscious or deliberate inference in perception and intuition. But there is implicit inference in both. The essence of each is to be found in its objective reference, and this reference is in the

[18] *The Two Sources of Morality and Religion,* pp. 237ff., 258ff.

nature of an inference from the subjective to the objective. Both perception and intuition are complex mental processes. Neither is an absolutely immediate apprehension of its object. All knowledge is mediated knowledge.

But mediation may be misleading. It often is. And hence there is a widespread feeling that the more immediate a conviction of reality is, the more trustworthy it is likely to be. This feeling, as we have seen, is hardly justified by the history of the scientific and philosophic criticism of sense experience. The tendency there has been to discredit more and more the affirmations of immediate sense experience. Yet there is still a residuum of objectivity which criticism has not succeeded in dissolving away; and the immediacy, with which this objectivity is apprehended, has no doubt been a factor in confirming belief in it. In any case there is a general feeling in religious circles that the more immediate and the more original the experience of God is, the better founded is the belief in him.

As a result of this feeling considerable dissatisfaction has arisen with the current psychological derivations of religious experience. These derivations have some of them had a hostile motive and on that account have awakened opposition. But for the most part they have had no such motive. They have been due to a purely scientific desire to trace the origin and development of religion. In carrying out this purpose some psychologists have found the source of religious faith in the human quest after life. Men feel themselves defeated in their struggle for that which they value above everything else and which they regard as a more or less obligatory goal, and so turn to a higher Power for aid. The belief in God thus arises as a supplement to human weakness. Other psychologists find the origin of religious experience in such emotions as subjection, fear, wonder, admiration, and awe —emotions awakened by extraordinary natural phenomena. These emotions are more or less social in character. They, consequently, led primitive men to personify the power or powers that caused the phenomena by which the emotions were evoked. In this way religious belief arose. It was due to the personifying tendency of the human mind stimulated by certain natural emotions.

These two theories have had wide vogue. They both seek to deduce religious experience from nonreligious sources. The process by which the transition from the nonreligious to the religious was made, may have been so spontaneous and immediate as to seem experiential rather than inferential in character. But an inference it nevertheless was. Because of their inability to attain the chief good of life or because of certain emotions they experienced men inferred the existence of a Divine Being or Beings. They may not themselves have been aware of the inference; but analysis clearly reveals it. And so an inferential theory of religious belief came to be widely held. Many, however, were dissatisfied with it. They felt that it was defective from the scientific standpoint. It failed to account for what is distinctive in religious experience. There is, they held, a unique element in the religious consciousness which cannot be deduced from natural or nonreligious needs or emotions. Then, what is more important, they regarded the theory as unsatisfactory from the apologetic point of view. It did not ground faith in religious experience, but deduced both faith and religious experience from more elementary forms of experience. And this, they felt, did not give our religious beliefs a sufficiently firm basis.[19]

This feeling of dissatisfaction with the current genetic explanations of religious experience is not wholly warranted, as we shall see later. But it has nevertheless been widespread. It was this feeling that lay back of Rudolf Otto's book

[19] For a valuable historical introduction to the modern scientific study of religious experience see *Recent Religious Psychology* (1928), by A. Rudolph Uren.

on *The Holy,* as it is called in the German, and gave such special interest to it. Professor Otto argued that the religious experience is primary and irreducible. It consists in an immediate apprehension of the Divine and cannot be analyzed into simpler elements or derived from them. This view was, of course, not new. It was a commonplace with the mystics, and might be said to be the cornerstone of Schleiermacher's theology. Schleiermacher laid great emphasis on the uniqueness of religion, defining it as "the feeling of absolute dependence." In this definition the word "absolute" is important. Religious experience is not simply one among a number of kindred feelings of dependence. It is a feeling of dependence on the Absolute and as such an altogether unique feeling. It stands apart from the other main interests of human life as a distinct and essential phase of human experience. "Only when piety," said Schleiermacher, "takes its place alongside of science and practice, as a necessary, an indispensable third, as their natural counterpart, not less in worth and splendor than either, will the common field be altogether occupied and human nature on this side complete."[20] "The feeling of absolute dependence," he declared, "is not an accidental

[20] *On Religion: Speeches to its Cultered Despisers,* translated by J. Oman, pp. 37f.

element, or a thing which varies from person to person, but is a universal element of life; and the recognition of this fact entirely takes the place, for the system of doctrine, of all the so-called proofs of the existence of God."[21] In other words, religious experience, or the consciousness of being in relation with God, is rooted so deeply in universal human nature and is such a unique and immediate mode of objective experience that it needs in theology no further confirmation than that furnished by the experience itself.

But while Schleiermacher thus insisted on the uniqueness, immediacy, and independent validity of religious experience, he did not, according to Otto, adequately ground his position. The distinction which he drew between "relative" and "absolute" dependence was "a difference of degree and not of intrinsic quality." Furthermore, the feeling of absolute dependence, as Schleiermacher conceived it, had primary reference to the self. It was "a category of self-valuation" or self-depreciation, the cause of which is to be found in God. But God came in secondarily. He was an inference from the feeling of dependence; and this, Otto declares, is the reverse of the truth. The ultimate feeling-element in religion "has indubitably in it-

---

[21] *The Christian Faith,* pp. 133f.

self immediate and primary reference to an object outside itself." The feeling of dependence is a consequence, not the cause, of the apprehension of the object. Our awareness of the object is "a primary immediate datum of consciousness." It precedes the feeling of dependence. "The latter presupposes the former, instead of the reverse."[22]

In this criticism of Schleiermacher and in his book as a whole what Otto seeks to do is to eliminate the inferential element from the objective reference of religious experience and to make our consciousness of the divine more immediate than psychologists generally have been willing to admit. In carrying out this purpose he coined a new term to designate the distinctive element in religious experience. He called it the "numinous," a word that he derived from the Latin *numen* (divinity), and to which he gave the meaning of an immediate awareness of the divine. It is to this numinous perception, he maintains, that the belief in God is to be ultimately traced. Our religious faith is not, then, an inference. It is based on immediate experience in the same way that our knowledge of the external world is. As the latter is developed out of *sensa,* so our knowledge of God is developed out of *numina*. *Numina* are as truly original

[22] *The Idea of the Holy,* pp. 9-11.

elements in experience as are *sensa*. As *sensa* constitute the raw material out of which the physical sciences are fashioned, so *numina* constitute the raw material out of which religious belief is built up. There is thus a close parallel between the development of scientific and of religious thought. Both follow essentially the same method, and in this respect equal validity may be claimed for both. Both are based on elementary psychical data.

This is not the whole of Otto's theory of religious knowledge, but it is the part that has appealed most strongly to the religious public and that has given his book such extraordinary vogue. It has been said that no other theological work since the *Speeches* or *Discourses* of Schleiermacher, published in 1799, has been read so widely in Germany as *The Idea of the Holy*. In it people have felt that a new and reassuring word concerning religion is spoken. They have found in it a powerful challenge to the current naturalistic explanations of religious experience. They have seen in it the immediacy of religious experience expounded in a way that seemed to bring new confirmation of its truth. But whether this popular appraisal of the book and its perceptual theory of religious knowledge is justified is a question that calls for further consideration.

Immediacy as a Test of Validity

Absolute immediacy, as we have seen, is impossible in our experience or knowledge of external reality, either finite or infinite. The claim to such immediacy by extreme mystics is unwarranted. Indeed, it is self-contradictory. No such claim appears in Otto's book. But there is a theory akin to it, held by strict empiricists. Representatives of this school have a good deal to say about "pure experience," and by this they mean "whatever has not been mentally elaborated." Professor Leuba tells us that he agrees with William James that such experience is invulnerable. "There is here no room for difference of opinion." But there is, he says, danger of confusing "pure experience with elaborations of it"; and this he thinks James has done in his apology for mysticism. He has read into pure experience far more than the actually "given" or "immediate."[23]

This idea of pure experience, however, is a sheer abstraction. It has no valid basis in either epistemology or psychology. "Pure" in the sense of unmediated experience of objective reality is a fiction; and equally untenable is the idea of an articulate experience that has undergone no

[23] J. H. Leuba, *The Psychology of Religious Mysticism,* p. 308.

mental elaboration. James himself tells us that apart from the work of thought the immediate sense life would be a "big blooming buzzing confusion." What transforms this confusion into articulate experience is a process of mental elaboration. Without the elaborating or interpreting activity of the mind there could be no knowledge of external reality. The objectively real can exist for us only as we think it. The idea that there is such a thing as pure "unassailable" experience, which passively mirrors objective reality, is a relic of pre-Kantian empiricism. Actual experience is constituted by thought and has no existence apart from it. Pure experience is as mythical as "the pure Nordic race."

But while the notion of absolute immediacy and that of a "pure" objective experience are untenable, there are different degrees of relative immediacy. The highest degree of the latter is what Rudolf Otto sought to establish for religion. He rejected the current genetic account of religious belief and also Schleiermacher's theory of its origin on the ground that they did not do justice to the immediacy of religious experience. They allowed a place to inference. As against this Otto argued for a direct apprehension of the religious object. But this directness, it is obvious, is not altogether free from an inferential element. It implies at least an inference from the subjective to the objective, and this inference is one whose validity is certainly as much open to question as is that of sense perception. Much sense perception is deception. The same is also true of religious perception or intuition. Numinous experience is no more "invulnerable" or "unassailable" than is sense perception.

Indeed, the objectivity of religious experience is not only as dubious as that of sense experience; it is psychologically much less compelling. Our sense impressions, no matter how misleading they may be, usually carry conviction with them. As Zeno put it, they "take hold of one by the hairs of one's head and drag one to assent." This could hardly be said of our ordinary religious experiences. The fact is that there are no concrete religious percepts such as we have in sense experience. Our religious impressions are as a rule vague in character and only dimly apprehend the more-than-human Object.

Then, too, religious experience is conditioned by subjective factors and by antecedent belief in a way and to a degree that sense experience is not. There are, it is true, subjective and interpretative elements in sense experience also; but they are less distinctly personal and valuational in character than is the case in religious experience. The *numina* of Rudolf Otto's theory, no matter how original and purely perceptual they may be, are manifestly valuational experiences in a way that the ordinary *sensa* are not. And as for the higher forms of religious experience, it is evident that they are to a large extent conditioned by antecedent belief. Some people have claimed for themselves direct experiences of the three Persons of the Trinity. John Wesley ran across several such. He speaks of nine or ten in London and three or four in Dublin. "Formerly," he said, "I thought this was the experience of all those that were perfected in love; but I am now clearly convinced that it is not. Only a few of these are favored with it."[24] That the experience was genuine in the cases referred to, Wesley did not apparently doubt; and there is no reason why we should question it. But it is evident that no one would have such an experience who was not acquainted with Christian theology. Christian theology is a source of Christian experience quite as much as Christian experience is a source of Christian theology. The two go together. Experiences that we call Christian or religious would not have been such but for a prior faith.

---

[24] *The Letters of John Wesley,* edited by John Telford, VII, p. 392.

It does not, however, follow from this that the objective reference of religious experience is necessarily any less valid than the objective reference of sense experience. Professor Leuba declares that "the immediacy of religious knowledge is illusory," because only subjective sensations and feelings are truly "immediate" experiences. But on this basis it is obvious that the immediacy of sensuous knowledge is equally illusory. For sensuous knowledge transcends subjective sensations and feelings as truly as does religious knowledge. And the act of transcendence involves faith in one case as well as the other. Sensuous and religious cognition are in this respect on a parity.

A common method of trying to break the force of this fact is to ascribe the trans-subjective reference of religious experience to self-suggestion, while assuming that the corresponding reference of sense perception is so overwhelmingly confirmed by common sense and science that there can be no serious doubt as to its essential validity. We expect, it is said, a certain religious experience and the experience comes as a result of the expectation. It is the expectation that gives rise to the experience, and hence the experience is illusory. That there is some truth in this contention can hardly be questioned. But it is obvious that there could be no expectation of a religious experience, if no one had previously had such an experience. It is the religious experience of others that awakens within us the expectation of a similar experience. The religious experience that comes to us individually may be due in large part to our expectation. But originally it was experience that gave rise to expectation, not the reverse.

Furthermore, it is clear, as Will Spens has pointed out, that present religious experience "involves more than antecedent expectation, that it depends on a belief as to the basis of the experience."[25] The belief may awaken within us an expectation, but the important thing is not the expectation but the belief, and the important thing about the belief is not simply that it is subjectively held but that it is true, that it sustains a special relation to reality. Confirmation of this position is to be found in the unexpectedness of grace. We pray for one thing, and the answer often comes in a quite different form. We do not receive what we expect, though what we receive may prove more effective than what we expected. This is a commonly recognized fact in the spiritual life, a fact that is manifestly out of harmony with the view that the experience in question is merely the outcome of expectation. Some sort of expecta-

[25] *Belief and Practice*, p. 35.

tion is no doubt a normal condition of religious experience, but it is not the cause of it.

The same is also to be said of the belief that underlies expectation. Without belief there would probably be no religious experience. Normal religious experience is conditioned by belief; but belief is not the cause of the experience. Some beliefs or doctrines, such as those of the Holy Spirit, the incarnation, and atonement, may be more favorable to the production of religious experience than others, but they do not determine the precise form that the experience will take. Concrete religious experience, while conditioned by expectation and belief, cannot be deduced from either. There is apparently at its root an objective factor analogous to the stimulus of sense experience. At any rate a purely subjective explanation of religious experience, such as that offered by the theory of autosuggestion, is inadequate. The *truth* of religious belief may very well be an even more essential factor in mediating religious experience than the expectation to which the belief gives rise. Psychological analysis does not at this point warrant a radical distinction between sense experience and religious experience. The latter may be objectively conditioned or caused as truly as the former.

The attempt to discredit religious experience

by referring it to self-suggestion is thus a failure. But it by no means follows from this that religious experience is objectively valid. It may apprehend its Object with the immediacy of sense perception, as Otto argues that it does, and yet be illusory. Perception both on the sense plane and in religion is often deceptive. Indeed, solipsism in philosophy and illusionism in theology are both theoretically possible. There is no logical bar to either. The reality of both the material and the spiritual world can be doubted. There is nothing in perceptual immediacy that guarantees the metaphysical reality of the object perceived. Immediacy and truth do not necessarily go together.

But while this is so, immediacy does as a rule carry with it assurance. If we have an immediate or direct experience of an object, we are more certain of its existence than if we arrive at our knowledge of it in an indirect way. This is as true of the religious as of a material object. A sound apologetic instinct thus lies back of the attempt to establish a perceptual theory of religious knowledge. Absolute certainty cannot be attained in this way. But we do have in the theory a basis for personal assurance. This assurance may not be logically grounded. It may be merely a subjective feeling. It may be certitude rather than certainty. But from the practical standpoint it may nevertheless be of the utmost importance. For what we need above everything else is faith in the things of the spirit. And it does not matter very much how this faith is produced so long as we have it in purity and vigor. Indeed, the production of it through feeling and direct experience is likely to be more effective than through any process of inference or reasoning. Hence, the preacher as a rule utilizes the former method. He seeks in every way he can to awaken within men the numinous experience, an immediate awareness of the divine. This experience validates itself. It does not convince others; and it may later disintegrate under criticism and lose its validating power with the experient himself. But so long as it lasts as a fresh and spontaneous experience it tends to verify itself, and nothing can completely take its place as a source of religious certitude.

It may also be noted that in the immediacy of this experience we have the only adequate explanation of the persistence of religion through the various stages of human development. If religion owed its origin to primitive fear, to primitive social conditions, to primitive self-suggestion, or to primitive ignorance, one would expect that it would be discarded as men moved to a higher stage of culture. The same would also hold of religion if it originated in a later stage of human development. One would expect that it would be cast aside as men advanced to a still higher cultural level. But this has not taken place. Religion has persisted throughout the whole of human history. It has at times declined in influence, but it has shown extraordinary recuperative power. It has been contemporaneous with every generation, and it has been such because as Mommsen said, "God is immediate to every age." There is a direct experience of him, which is as a well of water within the human soul springing up into eternal life. On no other theory can the marvelous persistence and ever-renewed vitality of religion be accounted for. It is, however, psychological, not metaphysical, immediacy that is here claimed for religious experience, and to which religious experience owes much of its self-verifying power.

CHAPTER III

VALUE AND TRUTH

THE popular empirical apologetic of our day rests on two main pillars. One is the immediacy of religious experience; the other is its value. The former engaged our attention in the preceding chapter; here we are to deal with the latter. That immediacy and value are commonly regarded as valid tests not only of religious truth but of truth in general, is obvious; and equally obvious is it that neither test is infallible.

Our previous study has made it clear that there is and can be no absolute or metaphysical immediacy that excludes the possibility of error in our experience of the world or of persons either human or divine. Knowledge is not imported into the mind through the impact of external objects. It is not a thing that can be transferred from one object to another, nor is it a passive mirroring of objective reality. It is a reaction on the part of the mind itself to external stimuli and as such is a purely mental event without parallel or meaning on the impersonal plane. No matter how close or intimate the relation of the mind to the external object may be, knowledge is an act that originates within the mind itself, and its validity is dependent upon the essential trustworthiness of the human reason. That our reason is trustworthy, cannot be demonstrated. We assume it, and on this assumption all knowledge rests. But the assumption may be mistaken; and even if the general trustworthiness of the human reason be admitted, it is still possible that in any particular act of perception or inference it may go astray. There is no immediacy, metaphysical or otherwise, that is able to bridge the gulf between thought and thing or idea and object so completely as to guarantee the absolute validity of our objective knowledge. The possibility of error remains open despite all our epistemological monisms.

Nevertheless, there is a psychological "immediacy" in objective experience that carries conviction with it. This immediacy cannot be explained away as illusory in the case of religious experience and accepted as valid in the case of sense experience. If it has epistemological value in the latter case, there is no necessary reason why it should not have it in the former. Suggestion and expectation, it is true, play a larger part in religious than in sense experience, but they do not create the objective reference of religious experience. At the most they determine to some extent the particular psychological forms that the experience takes. The objective reference is as original and immediate in religious as in sense experience. And the assurance that the apparent immediacy of the religious object carries with it has the right to be treated in the same way as the corresponding assurance in sense experience. It is to be accepted as valid in default of positive disproof. This, as a matter of fact, is the method actually followed by the human mind in all fields of human inquiry.

Immediacy, however, is not the only source of certitude. Another source is the appreciative or valuational side of experience. And in religion it is a question which is the more important. Some lay the primary stress on mystical immediacy, and others on the emotional and practical value of religion. The result has been the rise of two different types of religious philosophy; mysticism, on the one hand, and pragmatism, on the other. The first of these we have considered so far as it relates to the validity of religious experience. We now pass to a consideration of the second.

In pragmatism there is an interesting parallel to the mystical doctrine of absolute immediacy. As the extreme mystic solves the apologetic problem by claiming that he has an experience of

God so immediate as to be indubitable, so the extreme pragmatist achieves the same end by redefining truth in terms of value or utility. He does not simply maintain that value is the test of truth, he holds that it is the essence of truth. An idea that is useful is by that very fact true. Its truth is its utility. "The effective working of the idea and its truth are," we are told, "one and the same thing—this working being neither the cause nor the evidence of truth but its nature."[1] There is, therefore, in truth no objective reference, no transcendent element. Its meaning is limited to processes within the mind and consists in their accord with one another. There is no dualism of thought and thing or idea and object that needs to be transcended and that can be transcended only by faith, thus rendering all knowledge more or less dubious. Truth is constituted by subjective verification; and so far as the latter is concerned there is no necessary uncertainty with reference to it. The utility of an idea is open to direct inspection, and when this is established, its truth is also established. Applied to religious experience this means that we need raise no question with respect to its objective validity. Its practical value is its truth, and beyond that we need not go. To

[1] John Dewey. Quoted by J. B. Pratt, *What Is Pragmatism?* p. 93.

experience the value of religion is, therefore, as decisive evidence of its truth as is the mystic's experience of the Divine Presence.

But this short and easy apologetic manifestly does not carry us very far. Instead of being a support of faith it is really a surrender to skepticism. If religion is true only in the sense that it has emotional and practical value, it is obviously not true in the sense in which people generally understand truth. Purely subjective truth is not truth. It is the denial of truth. If the belief in God and his righteous rule is not true, religion is not true. Only confusion can result from the identification of the truth of religion with its emotional and social values. Such a reinterpretation of truth cancels truth instead of establishing it.

If value has any apologetic significance, it must be as a test or revelation of truth and not as constitutive of its essence. Value is not truth, but it may help us to determine what is true. This is the sense in which appeal is customarily made to the valuational side of religious experience. Religious belief works, it bears fruit, it enlarges, enriches, and sustains life; and because it does so, we infer that it is true. Its truth is verified by its value; and the verification takes place in experience itself. It is a spontaneous act of the human spirit. Men instinctively infer truth from value. This holds not only of religious beliefs but of beliefs in general.[2]

The Nature of Value

The question now arises as to whether this spontaneous and popular pragmatism has a valid basis. Are we warranted in concluding that a proposition is true because it has beneficial consequences? Is the practical fruitage of a belief evidence of its truth? Is religion true because it is useful? To these questions our dominant intellectual tradition has been inclined to give a negative answer. It is said, and truly, that interest often leads the judgment astray. We easily believe what we are glad to believe. Hence, we need to be on our guard against allowing feeling or desire a voice in deciding questions of fact or of existence. Reality is what it is, regardless of our attitude toward it. If we are to apprehend it correctly, we must divest ourselves of all interest except the desire to know the naked truth. True knowledge is disinterested knowledge.

Especially is this held to be the case in the field of science. Natural science in its ideal is passionless. Not only does it aim to free itself from personal bias, it seeks to divest itself even

---

[2] For an excellent exposition of this standpoint, see *Religious Certainty*, by Francis J. McConnell.

of human interest. It sees in nature no purpose and no worth. All is colorless existence. There is, of course, change, and change according to law, but it is purposeless change. There are no gradations of worth. Psychical fact has in and of itself no more value than physical fact. Both are parts of a vast mechanical system driven from behind, and have equal standing in it. One does not necessarily serve the other. Man is not the end of creation. There is no end or goal to the knowable universe. Teleology has no place in the field of pure knowledge. Pure knowledge recognizes only facts and their causal relations. It is phenomeno-centric or cosmocentric. It begins with the world, not with man. The anthropocentric standpoint of faith belongs to the uncritical and unscientific past. For the modern mind it has been rendered impossible by the double degradation that man has suffered at the hands of science. The Copernican astronomy deprived him of that central position in the universe which he had previously been supposed to occupy; and the Darwinian theory of evolution robbed him of that unique and absolute eminence which he had hitherto claimed for himself in the world of animate beings. Man from the standpoint of natural science must, consequently, take his place in the universe as one purposeless act among countless others. To make him the central fact of existence and to subordinate the rest of the world to his interests, is an unwarranted act of presumption on our part, and a distortion of reality. The real world, the world of pure knowledge, is a dehumanized world, a world without purpose and without distinctions of value.

Such is the intellectual tradition that has come down to us from naturalistic science. Viewed merely as a method of dealing with what may be called the quantitative aspects of nature this tradition has served and still serves an important purpose. It represents a distinct advance beyond the earlier anthropomorphic modes of thought. But as a total *Weltanschauung,* as a complete world-view, it runs counter to the profoundest convictions of the human spirit. And out of this conflict has arisen what has come to be known as the philosophy of value. This philosophy is not wholly new. Its roots go back to Socrates, Plato, and Aristotle, and even further. But in the modern world it has taken on a new and distinctive character. Its profoundest and most significant formulation is to be found in the Kantian philosophy. This we shall deal with in the next chapter. Here we are concerned with the more empirical treatment of the subject as represented by pragmatism and the general theory of value.

Our first inquiry has to do with the nature of value. What does value mean? What are its constituent elements? In what does its essential nature consist? What is involved in the mental act of valuation? In what sense may values be said to be objective? The answer to these questions may be briefly stated in four or five paragraphs.

1. It is generally agreed that values are relative to personality, and that they have their root in the affective-volitional nature. It is feeling and desire that give rise to value. Which of the two is the more fundamental in the valuation process is a question that has been debated not a little. Those are probably right who have argued in favor of feeling. But as a matter of fact feeling and desire are so intimately related to each other that one to some extent implies the other. There is no clear line of demarcation between them. One tends to pass over into the other, and both are involved in the definition of value. Indeed, the whole personality is to some extent involved in every act of valuation. We may then say with Professor Schiller that "value is a personal attitude, of welcome or the reverse, toward an object of interest";[3] or with Professor Höffding we may say that "whatever conduces to satisfaction or supplies a need

[3] *Encyclopedia of Religion and Ethics,* XII, p. 589.

has worth, or is a good."[4] Value is thus relative to personal interest. It is a subjective satisfaction due to the supply of a need or the gratification of a desire. In a word, it is psychological in nature, and would have no meaning apart from feeling and desire or apart from sentient experience.

2. Values are, nevertheless, not purely subjective. They imply the existence, either actual or hypothetical, of the object. "For feelings of value," said the Austrian scholar Meinong,[5] "it is essential that they be feelings of existence." "The predication of value," said W. R. Sorley, "implies or assumes something existing which can be said to possess the value; the true bearer of value is an existing reality or something conceived as an existing reality. Were there no existence there would be no value; value out of relation to existence has no meaning."[6] Valuation has thus an objective reference, as does perception. There is, however, this difference. The perceptual judgment may perhaps be purely existential, but not so the value-judgment. Value is not necessarily included in the idea of existence. It is, rather, a plus, something added to

[4] *The Problems of Philosophy,* p. 154.

[5] Author of *Psychologisch-Ethische Untersuchungen zur Werttheorie,* and *Ueber Annahmen.*

[6] *Moral Values and the Idea of God,* pp. 108f.

bare existence, and is sometimes spoken of as a "tertiary quality."

This designation is an unfortunate expression in a double respect. It suggests that values belong to a subphenomenal realm, a third layer of being, more remote from reality than the "secondary" qualities and subject to grave suspicion. If the "secondary" qualities are subjective, the "tertiary" qualities must be still more so. To call values "tertiary" qualities is, then, to leave them in a distant and precarious relation to objective reality. Furthermore, this mode of expression suggests that value, like other qualities, is a predicate inherent in the nature of the object, and so simply a "way of apprehending the object." This, however, is not the case. Value, if termed a quality, is a quality of an altogether unique kind. It is not a phenomenon, a manifestation of the object that reveals its existence. It is, rather, a metaphysical aspect of its being, the objective counterpart of what we mean when we say that an object ought to exist or is worth existing. This aspect of objective existence is manifestly one of which natural science takes no cognizance; and it may conceivably have no reality, it may be simply a shadow of the mind's own throwing. But that it actually is something more, is implicit in the value judgment itself. The value judgment as such contains an existential reference, and thus transcends pure subjectivity.[7]

3. Values are also objective in the sense that they are not entirely relative to the individual. They are embodied in institutions, customs, and laws, to which the individual must submit. They also take the form of moral, religious, and aesthetic ideals, ideals that are legislated into the very structure of the human mind. As individuals we do not make them, we find them. They are autonomous validities. They stand in their own right. They have a universal and normative character. They command our allegiance, and in this sense are as truly objective to the individual as are the values incorporated in the structure of human society.

4. A still further claim to objectivity on the part of values is to be found in the fact that they enter into our theoretical knowledge to a greater degree than is commonly supposed. There is no such sharp distinction as Kant drew between the pure reason and the practical reason. Practical considerations or valuational processes are to a large extent constitutive of the factual world. The world of science is not the disinterested creation of the human mind. Interest and purpose have had a great deal to do with it.

[7] See A. E. Taylor, *The Faith of a Moralist*, I, pp. 24-66; and *Value and Existence*, by N. O. Lossky and John S. Marshall.

Even logic is now coming to be looked upon as a science of value. Heinrich Rickert, the distinguished German philosopher, for instance, holds that all judgments are value judgments. For him there are no merely existential judgments. It is the "ought" of the judgment, he tells us, that alone lifts it into true objectivity. And the teaching of pragmatism is not so far removed from this. According to pragmatism, there is no merely "registering" intellect. All "facts" involve valuation; and the test of truth is to be found, not in its correspondence with a supposed external reality, but in its utility, in its verification in life, in its contribution to human welfare. Valuation thus plays a part in all objective knowledge. And if this be so, it is obvious that values are not to be thought of as purely subjective. They, as well as "facts," have objective significance.

The Value of Religion

Our concern, however, is not with values in general but with religious values. In discussing the latter it is important that we distinguish between intrinsic and instrumental values. Intrinsic values are values that are inherent in the very nature of religion and that are in a sense ends in themselves. These values may be reduced to two: the feeling of trustful dependence, and moral inspiration. Of these the former is the more fundamental and characteristically religious. Out of it come peace, confidence, hope, and joy; the basic religious emotions. It is because of faith in a Creator and Sustainer of the world that we are profoundly optimistic as we contemplate the future. It is because of our conviction that all is safe in the divine hands that we attain to peace and joy. This sense of security and of inner peace and contentment may, it is true, be carried to a one-sided extreme. It may lead us to take "moral holidays" to which we have no right; and against this we need to be on our guard. But when it is coupled with a resolute moral will, it is at once the profoundest and richest of religious values. It expresses itself in the assurance that in all the evils of human life we may be "more than conquerors through him that loved us," and in the conviction that we can do all things through Christ who strengtheneth us. This joyous confidence may or may not be warranted, but in any case it is the logical outcome of that trustful attitude toward God which is the inmost essence of religion.

With respect to the moral inspiration of religion there is some question as to whether it should be regarded as an "intrinsic" religious value. Many have argued that pure religion exhausts itself in the feeling of absolute dependence or in some other unique or distinctive mental state, and that its relation to morality is incidental or adventitious. That religion actually has been a great source of moral inspiration is not denied. But it is maintained by some that it has not always been such, and that it is not necessarily such, and by others it is contended that while religious belief normally manifests itself in good works, the latter belong to the fruits of religion rather than to religion itself. Religion in its essential nature is *extra-* or *supra-*moral.

This contention has significance by way of contrast with a purely moralistic theory of religion. There has always in the history of human thought been a tendency to identify religion with morality or treat it as a postulate of the moral nature. Immanuel Kant represented this tendency. He found the chief good of life in moral obedience and looked upon religion as an implication of the moral life. We must, he said, believe in God, freedom, and immortality; otherwise our moral nature would fall into contradiction with itself. But religious belief itself does not from his standpoint have an independent rational basis. It is a deduction from morality and ancillary to it. As such it serves an essential function in human life. It is a kind of moral necessity. But it is not self-sustaining. It draws its lifeblood from the moral nature. It is in morality that religion has both its source and its ground. God is a kind of device for getting us to do our duty.

This view has had considerable vogue; and as a corrective of its one-sidedness there is some justification for the opposite view that religion is radically distinct from morality, that its relation to the latter is secondary, and that moral inspiration is no essential constituent of religious experience. But however natural each of these views is as a reaction against the other, both are extreme. Religion is not a mere adjunct to morality, nor is it a compound of morality with emotion. It has its own distinctive nature. But it stands nevertheless in an intimate and essential relation to the moral life. If any evidence of this were needed, it would be sufficient to point to the Hebrew prophets. These men moralized religion; this is their permanent claim to distinction. They did so, however, not by introducing into religion an alien moral element, but by evoking from religion the moral element implicit in it. Religion without moral emphasis is embryonic and undeveloped. As it comes to spiritual maturity, it takes on increasingly an ethical character. It becomes, as Wesley used to say, "holy tempers." It manifests itself not simply as joy and peace but as love and righteousness. It stimulates as well as subdues the will. It transforms as well as saves men. And it does so by virtue of the moral ideals it imparts to men. These ideals are part and parcel of the religious view of the world; and the moral inspiration that results from them is properly to be regarded as belonging to the essence of religion. It is an intrinsic religious value.

These inner values of religion, which manifest themselves in a changed life, in a life of faith, hope, and love, constitute the heart of religion. Without them religion would lose its distinctiveness. But religion has also its "instrumental" values, and these have played an important rôle in human history. They are as complex and varied as life itself. They are social, economic, political, therapeutic, artistic, philosophical, educational, and cultural in character. They embrace every phase of human life. It is these values of religion that have appealed most to the secular world. Many, who have virtually no interest in personal religion and to whom the joy of the Lord means little or nothing, have prized highly the contributions of religion to social well-being and for this reason have supported the Church. Organized religion, it is true, has not always measured up to its opportunities. Grievous evils may justly be laid to its charge. It has not infrequently been a reactionary force. It has stood in the way of intellectual and social progress. There is some truth in the charge that organized religion has been "the opiate of the people" and that its ministers have been "the chloroforming agents of the confiscating classes." But evil as the influence of the Church has at times been, it has for the most part been a great humanitarian agency. It has been utilized for that purpose throughout all its history, and never more so than at present. Indeed, in some quarters so much emphasis has been placed on the instrumental values of religion that its intrinsic values seem to have lost much of their earlier significance. At this point there is real danger. The so-called social gospel should not, of course, be neglected, but it is still more important that the so-called individual gospel should not be overlooked. For if there is no individual gospel, there can be no social gospel. The latter is secondary, not primary. Neither, however, should be opposed to the other. When rightly understood, the two involve each other, and both are essential to the full-orbed Christian message.

What religion, at least in its Christian form, aims at is the furtherance of life, the creation and enjoyment of values. It has its own unique values; a peace that passeth understanding, a light not seen on sea and land. But it is also concerned with the light of common day, with peace and good will among men. It seeks to promote well-being as a whole. Its aim is fullness of life. Its values are as broad as human need and human capacity. In realizing these values it has, to be sure, fallen far short of its possibilities; but that it has on the whole made important contributions to their realization can hardly be denied. The very existence of religion through the centuries and through all the vicissitudes of human history is itself a most impressive testimony to its human worth. It is its value, both intrinsic and instrumental, that has kept it alive. Despite all its failures it has been and still is the salt of the earth.

The Empirical Argument From Value

We now recur to the question with which the present chapter is primarily concerned. Is there in the bare fact of its value any basis for affirming the objective validity of religion? Spontaneous thought, as we have seen, has no uncertainty on this point. It unhesitatingly deduces truth from value. But is it justified in so doing? Do the beneficial consequences of religious belief warrant our accepting it as true? Is valuational as well as perceptual experience cognitive? Does it reveal an objective order of reality? Not a few thinkers affirm that it does; and they base their conclusion on what they call empirical considerations. Indeed, with many the empirical argument for religion is simply an appeal to the practical value of religious belief. As illustrative of this type of thought the apologetic of three representative thinkers may be briefly outlined.

First and foremost is the religious pragmatism of William James. It is assumed by James that in the long run true beliefs work beneficially while untrue beliefs work perniciously. If we can, therefore, determine the practical consequences of a belief, we can decide whether the belief is true or not. If the belief in God "works" satisfactorily in the widest sense of the word, it is "true";[8] and so it is with religious beliefs in general. The problem of apologetics becomes thus a question of utility. If religion is useful, its truth follows as a matter of course; and whether it is useful or not is a question to which the answer can be found only in life. Life is the standard and test of truth. If religion promotes life, if it satisfies deep-seated needs of the human spirit, it by that very fact accredits itself. The living experience of its worth establishes its truth.

[8] William James, *Pragmatism,* p. 299.

In expounding this view James lays stress on the need of religion. The need is constitutional. We pray because "we cannot help praying."[9] It is the need of God that leads us to believe in him. We need him as a moral stimulus, as a releaser of our active energies. Without him we could not attain to "the most vigorous and most highly moral life." He is necessary as a postulate of our ethical nature. Then, too, we need him, not only as "inciter of our powers," but as himself a saving Power. We need him as Comforter, as Redeemer from our weakness and sinfulness. Our whole nature, both active and passive, cries out for the living God. And because of this fact, because of the way in which the belief in God responds to and satisfies the deepest needs of our nature, we are, according to James, justified in concluding that the belief is true.

But so far this is mere assertion, an expression of personal conviction rather than a reasoned conclusion. If we are to accept the underlying principle of religious pragmatism, some rational basis for it must be offered. And this James seeks to do by first pointing out that scientific as well as religious belief is subjective in its source and practical in its nature. An inner need underlies the belief in uniform laws of

---

[9] *Principles of Psychology,* I, p. 316.

causation as truly as it underlies the religious interpretation of the world. Indeed, "the conceiving or theorizing faculty . . . functions exclusively for the sake of ends that . . . are set by our emotional and practical subjectivity."[10] Scientific theories are all practical in their purpose and are judged by their practical value in the same way that pragmatism urges that religious beliefs should be. The latter "function in a practical manner and are tested by their results only in the sense in which all intellectual activity is ultimately practical."[11] The practical basis of religious belief is, therefore, no more of an argument against its validity than is the practical basis of scientific belief an argument against its validity. In both cases the beliefs are known as true or false by their fruits. Value is an index of objective reality.

This analogy, however, between religious and scientific beliefs did not, in James's opinion, go far enough. He felt the need of bringing truth and value closer together; and this he did by conceiving value not merely as a test of truth but as identical with it. In a word, he redefined truth in terms of value or utility. The truth of a belief thus became synonymous with its util-

---

[10] *The Will to Believe,* p. 117.

[11] J. S. Bixler, *Religion in the Philosophy of William James,* p. 94.

ity, so that to point out the value of religion was equivalent to establishing its truth. But truth, so defined, has manifestly no apologetic significance. It implies extreme skepticism, as we have already pointed out.[12] To some extent James seemed to realize this, for he did not wholly commit himself to the new theory. He hovered between it and the idea that utility is the test of truth without sharply distinguishing between them, and came to no final decision in favor of one as against the other. The real value of his apologetic lay in his broadening the base of valid argumentation so as to include in it not only strictly logical or theoretical considerations but also the emotional and volitional elements that figure so prominently in religious experience.

A somewhat different type of religious pragmatism is represented by Julius Kaftan. This distinguished Ritschlian theologian took his start from Kant. But he did not accept the Kantian theory of the categories. He was not an apriorist.[13] He was an empiricist in the sense that he regarded experience as "the sole source" of knowledge.[14] He was also a pragmatist in the sense that he held that "all knowledge in the last

---

[12] See p. 102.

[13] *Philosophie des Protestantismus,* pp. 134-144.

[14] *The Truth of the Christian Religion,* II, 17f.

resort is subordinate to the practical purposes of life."[15]

He differed, however, from William James in several important respects. For one thing he drew a sharp distinction between knowledge and faith. In harmony with Kant he limited "knowledge" to sense experience and to such "mental" experiences as constitute human history. It is experience, thus understood, that forms the basis of the special sciences; and to them knowledge is restricted. Everything beyond the limits of the empirical sciences belongs to speculation or to faith. It is not an object of knowledge. Knowledge is determined by objective fact. What is known is "something actually given, something real." In knowledge the free subjective factor is at a minimum. In faith, on the other hand, our own personal experience, our inner freedom, is the decisive thing. The will is here determinative. Between faith and knowledge the difference is thus so pronounced that we are not warranted in reducing them to a common practical function and arguing that the practical motive or faith underlying scientific knowledge is analogous to religious faith and that the latter is consequently as valid as the former. The common-sense view is correct that knowledge is knowledge and faith is faith.

[15] *Ibid.*, II, 316.

Out of this sharp distinction between faith and knowledge there arose a second point of difference between Kaftan and James. Both regarded experience as the sole source of knowledge. But experience, as Kaftan conceived it, is limited to the human and sense plane. There is, he held, no such direct mystical experience of the Divine as James argued for in *The Varieties of Religious Experience*. Nor is there anything in the merely human values of religious experience that warrants our affirming its objective validity. Utility is not necessarily a valid test of truth, and still less is it identical with truth. Experience as such, both sensuous and valuational, is limited to the phenomenal realm. It does not and cannot directly disclose transcendent reality. There can, therefore, be no strictly empirical justification or validition of religious belief. The empirical method is not applicable to the field of apologetics.

A third respect in which Kaftan differs from James has to do with the way they utilize the idea of value. According to James, the beneficial consequences of religious belief in general are valid evidence of its truth. He may lay more stress on one type of religious value than another, but all values resulting from religion he regards as forming a legitimate part of the apologetic argument. Not so, however, Kaftan. He looks upon religion as springing out of the quest after life. It has thus a practical source. But it was not the quest after the common goods of life that led to the rise of religion in the higher sense of the term. What gave birth to spiritual religion was the quest after the chief good. This is a quest that inevitably arises in human life. Temporal goods fail; and hence the human spirit seeks a higher good, a good beyond time and space, "a well of water springing up into everlasting life." It is in this idea of an eternal and absolute good that, according to Kaftan, not only the source and nature of religion but also its justification are to be found.

A fourth characteristic of Kaftan's religious pragmatism is its virtual limitation to the speculative realm, the realm of faith, as distinguished from the common experiences of life. Religion has, of course, its values for the life that now is. But these values are imperfect. They do not establish the truth of religion; they are, rather, the results of its truth. They are due to the belief in God, and hence cannot be the ground of this belief. The belief in God must have its source in the deepest intellectual and moral needs of the human spirit. There must be something in man that demands a knowledge that rises above the relative plane of science. There must be in him a demand for the Absolute. And that there is such a demand is attested by history. Individual men here and there may perhaps dispense with it, but human society cannot. It requires a supreme Idea. And this Idea can be consistently and rationally conceived only as an Idea of the chief good. A purely intellectual conception of the Absolute would be merely a duplicate of the present world. The highest knowledge must be cast in the mold of moral value. Reason itself demands this. No other view of the superworld will suffice. The Idea of the chief good is "the rational, the only and absolutely valid, Idea."[16] And this Idea, it is argued, has received its most perfect expression in "the Christian idea of the kingdom of God as the chief good of humanity." In the kingdom of God the religious and moral points of view are united in the closest manner with each other, and in this union we have the key to ultimate reality. Reason as embodied in our moral and religious nature requires a theistic view of the world. But it is only the practical reason of which this is true. The theoretical reason fails us when it comes to that which is most essential in religion, the idea of the Absolute. Here our only trustworthy guide is the idea of the chief good.

Such in brief is the pragmatic apologetic of

[16] *The Truth of the Christian Religion*, p. 224.

the Ritschlian school, as represented by Julius Kaftan. It is based primarily on the religious need of a belief in the Absolute and on the "rational" necessity of a practical or personal conception of the Absolute. Both the religious need and the rational necessity enter into what *we* call "religious experience." But Kaftan as a rule limits "experience" to the human and sensuous plane and hence speaks of faith rather than of religious experience. So far as he uses the latter term and identifies it with faith, he emphasizes its rational implications rather than its perceptual or intuitional character. God from his standpoint is a postulate of religious experience rather than its direct object.

The third type of religious pragmatism above referred to is that of Eric Waterhouse.[17] This English Wesleyan scholar represents a point of view that may be described as midway between the postulatory theory of Kaftan and the utilitarian theory of James. He leans toward the latter in his general epistemology; but in his emphasis on the collective religious experience of mankind he takes a step toward the semi-Kantian epistemology of Kaftan. He begins his apologetic by arguing that religion is "a normal predicate of the human mind," that it has "fos-

[17] *The Philosophy of Religious Experience*, 1923; *Psychology and Religion*, 1930.

tered qualities essential alike to the development of a stable social order and a fuller personality," that it has been the chief stimulus to human progress, and that there is "a universality and a kind of inevitability" about it that gives it "philosophical significance." As an empiricist he assumes that we come to know reality only through experience, and then maintains that since religion is an important and constituent factor in experience there is no reason why we should not find in it "an indication of the character of reality." The very fact that it has played such a commanding rôle as it has in human experience is presumptive evidence of its validity.

But before any definite conclusion can be drawn from this general consideration it is obvious that we need to know what is implied in religious experience with respect to reality. To this question Waterhouse devotes special attention, and concludes that the essential postulate of religion is "the existence of a divine-human relationship." Religion, he says, assumes that there is a superhuman order and that this "order is approachable, conciliable, that it is possible to establish a harmonious relation with it." Or, in philosophical terms, it assumes that "there is within reality that which is sympathetic to human values." There is "a harmony between reality and the ultimate value of all human existence." As much as this we must believe if we are to be truly religious. Even in atheistic Buddhism more or less of this belief is implied, as is evident from the doctrine of Nirvana.

We may then regard the belief in a fundamental harmony between existence and value as the minimum postulate of religious experience. But before the postulate can be accepted as valid, it needs verification. And here the question arises as to whether verification is possible in view of the fact of evil. In meeting this question Waterhouse points out that natural evil cannot be proved to be ultimate. It may serve a spiritual purpose, and manifestly often does. Indeed, it is only when the religious postulate is clearly conceived and firmly held that pain becomes a problem. For the unbeliever there is no problem of pain; the problem exists only for the believer. This is a significant fact. It points to two conclusions: first, that a practical solution of the problem is possible; and, second, that God looks upon pain differently from what we do.

If the problem of suffering arises only within the framework of faith, if it is faith that generates the problem, it is inherently probable that faith will also have its own way of dealing with it. It will solve the problem in such a way as to maintain its own vitality. That it has actually done so in the past is abundantly attested by history. Suffering has not destroyed faith. It has often strengthened it. It has done so because to the eye of faith there is no necessary antithesis between the divine goodness and the divine power. The divine goodness may manifest itself in and through pain. How, or why it should do so, we may not know; but faith at this point transcends the limitations of human knowledge and ascribes to God a different view of pain from that of the natural man. Such a difference of standpoint between the human and the divine is manifestly possible. It involves no contradiction and hence there is in the fact of evil no insuperable barrier to the acceptance of the religious postulate.

Nor is any such barrier to be found in Agnosticism or Pessimism. There is no way of proving that we can know nothing concerning ultimate reality, and still more impossible is it to prove that there is a fundamental dissonance between reality and human value. These two philosophical attitudes are discredited by experience. Only on this ground can we account for the limited extent to which they have been accepted, and for "the overwhelming preponderance of the religious postulate."

It is to experience, according to Waterhouse,

that we must go for the confirmation of any postulate; and it is here that the religious postulate finds its verification. "The religious postulate works better in experience than the postulate of a neutral reality. It explains more. It helps mankind to face pain and sorrow. It gives meaning to life and tonic to moral effort."[18] In these facts we have the key to the continuity of religion. Religious belief has met permanent human needs, and for this reason has persisted despite all opposition. "There never has been truly an age of unbelief." Prayer has always sprung spontaneously to human lips, and in the opinion of the great majority of men has been justified by its fruits. It is so also with religion as a whole. The place it has filled in human history is its justification. "The persistence of the religious point of view is the best evidence of the verification of its postulate."

The mere idea of an ultimate harmony between existence and value, however, is rather vague. Something more definite is implied in religious experience. There is in it a sense of communion with reality. And communion implies similarity of nature, similarity between ourselves and the causal ground of the world. We may, therefore, on the basis of our own personality and our own religious experience speak

[18] *The Philosophy of Religious Experience,* p. 190.

of God as personal in the sense that he is "a responsive God," a God responsive to our needs and to our intelligence. It is also implied in religious experience that God is good, that we can trust him. Without these implications religious experience would lack definiteness of content and clearness of direction. It is the personality and goodness of God that alone make possible a full expression of the religious consciousness. In them we may, consequently, according to Waterhouse, see "highly justifiable corollaries of the postulate of religious experience."

The three types of pragmatic apologetic, which have been briefly outlined, represent somewhat different points of view, but underlying them all is the common assumption that religious experience is not purely subjective, that it reveals to some extent the nature of objective reality, and that the validity of this revelation is verified by its practical value. The value is somewhat differently conceived in each instance. James lays stress on the general utility of religion and on its moral and emotional value to the individual. Kaftan emphasizes the moral and spiritual necessity of the belief in God and the unique and profound satisfaction that results from it. Waterhouse dwells on the collective value and historical significance of religion. But in each case it is the worth of religion that is regarded as the convincing evidence of its truth. In elaborating this point of view James and Waterhouse attach considerable significance to the kinship between the valuational process which underlies scientific knowledge and that which underlies religious knowledge. Kaftan, on the other hand, draws a sharp distinction between the theoretical character of scientific knowledge and the practical character of religious knowledge. Indeed, he is inclined to oppose religious faith to scientific knowledge and to emphasize the qualitative distinctiveness of religious values rather than their quantitative importance in human life as a whole. This, however, is a difference of method and emphasis rather than of fundamental standpoint. At bottom all three mean essentially the same thing.

The Value of the Pragmatic Argument

The pragmatic argument, especially as developed by James and Waterhouse, makes a strong appeal to the popular mind. It reflects the way the average man thinks. The first question that most people ask with reference to any belief submitted to them for consideration has to do with its practical value. Will its acceptance profit them or profit people in general? If they think it will, they will almost inevitably be prejudiced in its favor. They will look upon the belief as probably true. In many instances there will naturally be differences of opinion as to whether a particular belief is actually profitable or not. The facts may be ambiguous. Some may point in one direction and some in another. Or, what is perhaps more common, the same facts may admit of different interpretations. People have different standards of value, and, consequently, appraise facts and beliefs differently. To some, for instance, the belief in immortality seems a moral opiate, a means of dulling the social conscience and of perpetuating social evils, a bar to social progress. To others it is the source of all high moral inspiration, the one adequate ground of faith, hope, and love. The difference between these two groups is manifestly one of moral standard and of spiritual insight. And until this difference is overcome, the consequences of the belief in immortality and of religious beliefs in general will necessarily be differently estimated. But in so far as these consequences are judged beneficial by the common standards of the day, there can be no doubt that the tendency will be to see in them evidences of the truth of religion. The human mind is pragmatic in its bent.

Of this fact the preacher has naturally and properly taken advantage. He has appealed to the practical values of religion as sufficient ground for accepting its beliefs. He has judged religious doctrines by their fruits rather than by their logical or philosophical consistency; and he has done so because he has found it the most effective method of influencing people in general. This was strikingly characteristic of Wesley. In defending his doctrine of conversion he said: "I have seen (as far as a thing of this kind can be seen) very many persons changed in a moment from the spirit of fear, horror, despair, to the spirit of love, joy, and peace; and from sinful desire, till then reigning over them, to a pure desire of doing the will of God. These are matters of fact, whereof I have seen, and almost daily am, an eye or ear witness. . . . That such a change was wrought appears . . . from the whole tenor of their life, till then many ways wicked; from that time holy, just, and good. I will show you him that was a lion then, and is now a lamb; him that was a drunkard, and is now exemplarily sober; the whoremonger that was, who now abhors the very 'garment spotted by the flesh.' These are my living arguments for what I assert."[19] And these have always been the most convincing arguments in the propagation of the Christian faith. It was the moral transforma-

[19] *Journal,* May 20, 1739. For a similar passage see his *Letters,* vol. II, p. 290; quoted by Umphrey Lee, *John Wesley and Modern Religion,* p. 142.

tions wrought by the Evangelical Revival of the eighteenth century more than anything else that led to the rapid spread of the movement throughout the churches of England and America and to its present world-wide influence. When religion manifests itself in demonstration of the Spirit and of power, it has as a rule little difficulty in convincing the intellect.

But while this is probably true, the question nevertheless arises as to whether the intellect is justified in yielding to moral and spiritual pressure. Is it warranted in inferring validity from value? Are the beneficial consequences of religious belief adequate evidence of its truth? May we legitimately and honestly believe in religion on the basis of its practical value alone?

In answering this question we are at first confronted with the humanistic claim that the same values, the same high experiences, that are evoked by devotion to God, may be and are evoked by devotion to man, and that the valuational aspects of religious experience consequently have no apologetic significance. They do not necessarily involve such a postulate as Waterhouse finds in them. The theistic inference is read into them rather than out of them. It is a useless appendix rather than an essential ingredient. In this connection much stress is at present laid on the moral enthusiasm and social idealism generated by Communism, especially in Russia; and by many the belief is expressed that in such a purely humanistic and naturalistic movement we have a moral equivalent of historical religion and an adequate substitute for it. The same moral and spiritual inspiration, it is urged, can be awakened by the contemplation of humanity as by the contemplation of a personal God and Father of us all.

This theory is in principle not new. It is a revival in modified form of Comtean positivism or the Religion of Humanity. It may or may not call itself a religion, but in either case it seeks to occupy the place hitherto occupied by what it regards as the discredited faiths of the past. For all practical purposes it is a religion without God. It tries to secure the benefits of religion without religion. This attempt has often been made; it is renewed in almost every generation, and always with the same futile result. Theoretically there may be no conclusive reason why humanism should not evoke a moral devotion akin to that of theism. But actually it has not done so. It is theistic religion that through the ages has been the great generator of moral idealism and of moral enthusiasm. What capacity an independent and self-sufficient humanism would have in this respect we do not know. Nor is there any way in which we could find out. Before humanism could really be put to the test, human life in general would need to be pretty thoroughly dereligionized; and whether this will ever take place or is even possible, is open to serious question. In any case religion is still a vital power the world over, and so long as it remains such, there is no way of determining what degree of moral inspiration, if any, an independent humanism would have. The truth would seem to be that the humanistic faith is an offshoot from Christianity, a Christian heresy, and that it derives its moral strength from the very faith it denies. It is a parasitic growth and without the mother-soil of historical religion would soon perish. Its criticism of the pragmatic argument need not, therefore, be taken very seriously.

Another objection to the argument comes from a certain type of psychologist. He argues, not that humanity could serve the same function in religious experience as God, but that the inspirational value of the religious Object is not dependent upon *his* or *its* existence. If people *believe* that God exists and that they truly experience him, it does not matter whether he actually exists or not. In either case the beneficial effects would be the same. It is the *belief* in God that is the important thing. The God believed in may be purely imaginal or conceptual,

He may not be metaphysically real. Yet if he is believed to be real, the consequences will be the same, no matter whether the belief be valid or not. All that we can, therefore, logically deduce from the moral and spiritual inspiration of religion is the practical value of the belief in God viewed merely as a psychological fact. The belief in and of itself is sufficient to account for the beneficial consequences of religion, and beyond that we cannot go. No pragmatic proof of the divine existence, no proof based on purely practical considerations, is possible.[20]

From the strictly psychological or scientific point of view this is no doubt true. But the objection would hold equally against all forms of belief. It would apply to sense experience as well as religious experience. There is, as we have repeatedly pointed out, no absolutely immediate knowledge of objective reality. Virtually all so-called knowledge is ultimately belief. The only question that concerns us is as to whether the belief is valid or not. We have various tests of validity, and among these is that of utility. The utility of a proposition cannot transform it from a belief into absolute knowledge. It cannot transcend the dualism of thought and thing or idea and object. But it may conceivably serve as an indication or test of objective valid-

[20] See F. R. Tennant, *Philosophical Theology,* I, pp. 304f.

ity. And our question is as to whether such a use of it is logically justified. In other words, does the principle of pragmatism have metaphysical validity? To this question psychology has no answer either negative or affirmative. It cannot itself go beyond the subjective fact of belief and its utility. The ontological lies beyond its domain.

That value is a revelation of reality is a metaphysical assumption, and an assumption that implies a theistic world view. In a world ruled by a good God we should expect that true beliefs would as a rule have beneficial effects, while the reverse would hold for error and illusion. But if there is no God, there is no inherent reason why an erroneous belief should not yield beneficial results. From a materialistic or atheistic standpoint religious beliefs might have all the practical values claimed for them, and yet they would be regarded as illusions. It is only on a theistic basis that there is a necessary connection between truth and value. The pragmatic principle, that a belief is verified by its utility, presupposes the view that the ruler of the world is a lover of truth. In other words, pragmatism is implicit theism. William James tells us that, if the belief in God works satisfactorily, it is true. But it is such only for him who already believes there is a God. If there were no God, the fundamental principle of pragmatism would be an arbitrary and inconsistent assumption.

It is, therefore, clear that the pragmatic argument in its empiricistic form brings us to nothing final. It starts with the acknowledged fact that people are predisposed in favor of any belief that proves itself of practical value. But whether this psychological predisposition is logically warranted and a safe guide to truth, is a question that is not adequately answered. The radical pragmatist seeks to solve the problem by equating truth with utility, but in so doing he destroys truth and falls into an all engulfing skepticism. The more moderate religious pragmatist points out that valuational processes are involved in scientific theories as well as religious beliefs, and concludes that this fact is favorable to the validity of the latter. But no profound and clearly defined theory of religious knowledge is developed. Things are left pretty much at loose ends. No sharp line is drawn between the psychological and the logical treatment of the subject. Appeal is made to popular feeling rather than critical thought. This follows naturally from the standpoint adopted. Empiricism and pragmatism do not permit one to recognize "faculties of knowledge and potentialities of thought in the spirit itself"; and so long as one is debarred from so doing he is unable to deal satisfactorily with the deeper aspects of the problem of knowledge. Much that the religious pragmatist says may be true and valuable, but he does not strike bottom.[21]

[21] For a summary criticism of pragmatism as a system of philosophy, see my *Philosophy of Personalism,* pp. 397-407.

CHAPTER IV

THE PRINCIPLE OF SELF-VERIFICATION

IMMEDIACY and value are the two factors that contribute most to belief and conviction. This holds true of both sense experience and religious experience. In the latter value is perhaps the more important factor. It is the worth of religion rather than the conscious immediacy of its Object that with most people leads to belief. But both factors are vital elements in religious faith; and so we have both a perceptual or mystical and a valuational or pragmatic theory of religious experience.

These two theories were the subjects of discussion in the two preceding chapters. Neither theory, as we have seen, has a decisive bearing on the question of the validity of religious experience. Both are psychological rather than logical theories. They describe the verifying processes which actually influence people rather than those which logic would dictate.

The immediacy we ascribe to experiential knowledge is apparent rather than real. There is in objective knowledge no such thing as absolute or metaphysical immediacy. All cognition is mediated, and hence is exposed to the possibility of error. Indeed, most sense perception is deception. Things are not as they seem. This has been strikingly demonstrated in the history of human thought by the scientific distinction between primary and secondary qualities, by the Copernican theory of astronomy, and by the current electronic theory of matter. As a result of the acceptance of these theories about all that now remains of the material objects of sense perception is atomic centers of force, modes of being wholly different from what they appear to be. And if sense perceptions are so misleading, it is obvious that religious perceptions may be equally if not more so. For they are as a rule far less definite in character, and vary to a larger degree from individual to individual. In some instances, as with the mystics, they take the form of a distinct sense of Presence; but with most people they do not emerge above a vague consciousness of an invisible and supernatural existence. Whether such a consciousness may properly be said to be perceptual is open to question. In any case it carries with it no compelling conviction. The definitely "mystical" experience is different. Here there is a convincing sense of objectivity. But this experience has little if any evidential value for those who have not had the experience. To them it seems illusory or at least of questionable validity.

Value is also an uncertain criterion of truth. To identify truth with value or utility, as some pragmatists do, would be suicidal. It would mean the destruction of truth itself. Truth is one thing and utility is another. To equate the two would lead only to confusion and error. This, however, does not mean that there is no relation between them. Some truths are manifestly useful. In a general way it may also be said that true beliefs bring one into harmony, and false beliefs into conflict, with reality, so that good results in one case and evil in the other. But the matter is not actually so simple as all this. Comparatively few beliefs have a direct and obvious bearing on physical well-being. This is particularly true of such "over-beliefs" as those of religion. Some of these beliefs no doubt have a therapeutic value. But very few if any would put the case for their validity on this basis alone. It is other and higher values to which the religious pragmatist appeals. And this appeal carries weight with most people. But whether it ought so to do, is a question.

Many see in religious belief simply a case of "wishful thinking." This is the conclusion to which a naturalistic philosophy logically leads. According to this type of thought there is no fundamental harmony between value and truth. The assumption that there is, is merely a relic of an outmoded spiritualism. Pragmatism, in so far as it serves as a religious apologetic, is an attenuated theism. It assumes—what only a theist is warranted in assuming—that there is a basal harmony between value and truth, and then argues that the emotional and general utilitarian values of theistic belief are evidence of its truth. It thus clearly begs the question. It proves what it has already assumed. It bases its theistic argument on a theistic assumption; and the assumption is grounded in wishful thinking. We want to believe that the higher spiritual values of life are the key to the nature of reality and so assume that they are. The assumption is simply an objectification of desire. There is nothing in the nature of reality that requires or justifies it. Religion may have all the practical values attributed to it and yet be an illusion. The so-called "truths by which we live" may be and probably are fictions.[1]

So it seems to the naturalistic philosopher; and to this line of reasoning there is no adequate response on a pragmatistic and empiricistic basis.[2] If we are to present the case for religious

---

[1] See H. Vaihinger, *The Philosophy of 'As If.'*

[2] Some good illustrations and also expositions of the inadequacy and inconclusiveness of the pragmatistic and empiricistic types of religious apologetic are to be found in the recent volume of essays, entitled *The Nature of Religious Experience,* by several former students of D. C. Macintosh.

experience in an effective and convincing manner, we must approach the subject from a profounder point of view. We must take our start, not from William James, but from Immanuel Kant. We must begin, not with experience as ultimate, but with the question, How is experience possible? And in answering this question we must give proper recognition to the subjective conditions of experience. Experience is not an objective entity that can be passed from mind to mind. The mind is not a blank tablet on which the contents of experience are written by some extraneous hand. It is not an empty receptacle into which experience can be poured from without. Experience is itself a mental product and apart from the activity of the mind would have no existence. The human mind, to be sure, is a dependent being and is conditioned in its activity by external stimuli. But these stimuli are the occasion, not the cause, of the activity. The activity is mental, not material. It has its own distinctive nature; it is not a modified form of physical energy. It accompanies cerebral activity, but is not produced by it. Nor does it owe its origin in any proper sense of the term to experience as ordinarily understood, either racial or individual. Experience, it is true, does influence mental development. But in the last analysis it is not experience that produces the mind but the mind that produces experience. Without the constitutive activity of thought there could be no articulate experience. The first prerequisite of experience is a creative mind.

In the next place it should be noted that the mind is not only creative but creative along four fundamentally distinct lines and that these different lines of creative activity give rise to four different kinds of experience. There is sense experience, there is religious experience, there is moral experience, and there is aesthetic experience. Each of these types of experience is grounded in human nature. Man has a native capacity for each of them. This capacity is variously named. It is spoken of as a faculty, an interest, an a priori, a faith. But it matters not what it is called so long as it is recognized as an immanent principle or endowment of the human mind and so long as each of these capacities is seen to be distinct from the others. Numerous efforts have been made to deduce one from another or from something simpler as, for example, the religious from the nonreligious and the moral from the nonmoral; but all these efforts have failed. The four fundamental capacities of the human spirit are structural in human nature or in human reason. They are unique and underived. One cannot be reduced to another.

Each is inherent in man as a rational spiritual being.

In defining these a priori capacities of the human spirit it should be clearly fixed in mind that they are purely *formal* in character. They have no specific or concrete content. They are not innate ideas. They do not exist as distinct conceptions anterior to or independent of experience. They manifest themselves in and through experience. Without experience they would not reveal themselves, they would be completely hidden from view. It is through experience that we come to know them or to infer their existence. And, on the other hand, if they did not exist, there could be no experience. It is these hidden powers of the soul that make experience possible. They are its creative source. They react in certain definite ways to external stimuli and through this reaction generate and build up our human experience.

A distinction is at times drawn between the structure of experience and its raw material or between its form and its content, and it is assumed that the creative activity of the mind has to do only with the structure or form. The raw material or content is "given"; we passively receive it, and the mind then works it up into articulate or rational form. This in large measure is a correct description of what takes place.

But it is a mistake to draw a sharp distinction between the formal structure of experience and its material content. Both go together. There is no experience that may properly be described as formless content and none that may be correctly described as contentless form. The two conceptions are abstractions. There is more or less of both form and content in all actual experience. And both the formal structure and the material content are mental products. "The affections of the sensibility" are not purely passive. They involve mental activity as truly as do the rational forms of experience. Experience as a whole owes its origin to the innate capacities of the human spirit. These capacities are not only "formal," they are "formative." They are the creative sources of all the great types of human experience. They are, it is true, evoked by external stimuli and conditioned in their development by the physical and social environment, but they nevertheless determine the essential nature and main directions of human experience. Without them experience in all its essential forms, sensuous, religious, moral, and aesthetic, would be impossible.

The Religious Nature of Man

It is in the light of such a conception of the human mind that any profound inquiry into the validity of religious experience must be conducted. We must begin by raising the question as to the possibility of religious experience and must find the answer in a unique endowment or potentiality of the human spirit. It is at this point, in my opinion, that the most significant contribution has been made to the philosophy of religion and to empirical apologetics in modern times.

There is a Latin maxim to the effect that there is nothing in the intellect which was not previously in sense. John Locke as an empiricist adopted this maxim, and his great rationalistic contemporary, Leibnitz, also endorsed it, but only on the condition that it be supplemented by the clause, "Except the intellect itself." Without this supplement the aphorism is misleading. It suggests that the intellect is simply a passive recipient of a ready-made knowledge, when as a matter of fact it is a constitutive factor in all knowledge and in all articulate experience. It "is organic, and when it acts, it acts in accordance with its own constitution and laws."[3] If it had no constitution, no distinctive nature of its own, if its functions were all determined from without, it would be virtually nonexistent. The real existence of the mind means that it has its own definite and distinct nature

[3] B. P. Bowne, *Theory of Thought and Knowledge*, p. 349.

and that this nature is a determining factor in knowledge.

It was this insight that lay back of Kant's epoch-making work. What this greatest of modern thinkers sought to do was to analyze thoroughly the human mind and to ascertain, if possible, the contributions it makes to experience and knowledge. In carrying out this purpose he distinguished between the "pure" or theoretical reason and the "practical" reason. Each of these he subjected to a profound and searching criticism. The net result of this criticism was embodied in the two great principles of the creative activity of thought and the primacy of the practical reason. These principles gave a new direction to philosophic inquiry and became the basis of modern idealism.

The particular way in which Kant developed the idea of the creative activity of thought does not at present concern us. There was much that was technical and academic in his method. His system of the categories is for us outmoded. But the essential idea underlying it is sound, and despite all criticism remains "a permanent possession of reflective thought."[4]

Perhaps as clear and convincing an exposition of the essential Kantian teaching at this point is to be found in the systematic works of Borden

[4] B. P. Bowne, *Personalism,* p. 56.

P. Bowne[5] as anywhere. He classified the categories under two heads: the phenomenal and the metaphysical. Under the former he included time, number, space, motion, and quantity. Of these the first two are involved in all phenomena. Our mental states themselves as well as the objects of experience stand in temporal and numerical relations to each other. The other three categories—space, motion, and quantity—apply only to sensuous objects. These objects not only succeed each other in time and are capable of being numbered; they stand in spatial and quantitative relations to each other and move from place to place. Whether these various relations that inhere in mental and physical phenomena have an extramental existence or not, is a question that does not here concern us. In either case these relations can exist for us only as we think them. It is the phenomenal categories with which the human mind is endowed that make possible our temporal and spatial experiences.

Under the metaphysical categories Bowne included being, quality, identity, causality, and purpose. Of these purpose belongs to the higher ranges of thought. It is needed for the more complete systematizing and unifying of our objects. But this need manifests itself clearly only

---

[5] See especially *Theory of Thought and Knowledge*, pp. 59-116.

in reflective thought. Elementary experience does not disclose it to any marked extent. When we take things as they appear in sense perception, it is easy to disregard the category of purpose altogether and hence to call in question its validity. It seems on this plane to stand in no essential relation to reason. Its necessity or rational significance becomes clear only when thought becomes systematic and aims at completeness.

The other metaphysical categories are structural in our elementary objective experience. Without the categories of being, quality, identity, and causality there could be no experience of the world or of an objectively existing order. In the idea of the world, of the soul, and of God all these categories are involved. They are essential to the conception of reality itself. An object is metaphysically real only in so far as substance, quality, identity, and causality can be ascribed to it. And the ascription is, of course, the work of the mind itself.

The categories, both metaphysical and phenomenal, are not at the outset conscious possessions of the mind. They may become such later as a result of the mind's reflection on its own work. But at first and in their normal operations they are immanent mental principles. They are like the muscles of the body which we use in walking but of whose existence we are not directly conscious. Or they are like the immanent and invisible law of growth without which the unfolding of the organism could not be understood. They manifest themselves in the products of thought and we discover them through analysis. But, like the law of growth, they are unpicturable. They are not the instruments of thought nor mental compartments. They are, rather, organic principles which determine the form of knowing and through which experience is built up. They are not separate faculties; they are merely variant modes of activity. The reality is always the one mind acting in different ways. It is this truth that underlies the Kantian theory of the categories. The theory emphasizes the fact that the mind is unitary, that it is active, not passive, and that objective experience is not imported ready-made from without but is the product of a complex mental activity which has its own forms and principles.

As a distinct creative activity of the mind thus underlies sense experience and makes it possible, so a similar activity, according to Kant, underlies and makes possible moral experience. The latter activity is attributed to the practical reason, as the former is to the theoretical reason. This, of course, does not mean that there are two independent "reasons" within the human mind.

There is, rather, one reason operating in two different fields or in two different ways. But the two methods or the two fields are sufficiently distinct to make it permissible to speak of both a "theoretical" and a "practical" reason.

The theoretical reason is made up of the various categories or a priori principles to which we have referred and as many more as may be necessary to express the different forms of mental activity. In one respect we might say that the knowledge of anything and everything is a priori. It is such in the sense that it is not passively received from without but involves a special activity of the mind. These activities, however, fall into certain classes, and the process of classification may be carried to a point where the different classes become incommensurable and defy further reduction. When this is done, we have "the elementary and essential principles of intelligence"; and these principles may be called "categories," as expressive of the fundamental forms of mental action. But in and of itself there is no necessary limit to the number of categories. We may have as many or as few as we wish provided they represent distinct forms of mental activity and do not put incommensurable things together.

The structure of the practical reason is not so complex as is that of the theoretical or speculative reason. There are not so many fundamental principles or categories involved in it. We may distinguish three or four. First is the obligation to do the right and avoid the wrong. This obligation presupposes the recognition of a radical difference between right and wrong. Both the recognition and the obligation have their source in the moral nature itself. They cannot be deduced from anything simpler. They are due to a native capacity for moral distinctions and to the autonomous action of the human spirit in imposing duty upon itself. Beyond this native capacity and autonomous action we can not go. They are inherent in free intelligence itself. They are a priori endowments of the human mind.

A second category of the practical reason is the law of good will. "There is nothing in the world," said Kant, "which can be termed absolutely and altogether good, a good will alone excepted."[6] This insight stands in its own right. It needs no proof. The relation that ought to exist between personal beings everywhere is that of love or good will. There is no other law having to do with the interaction of moral beings so universal as this. Whenever and wherever two or more persons meet under normal conditions,

[6] *The Metaphysic of Ethics,* p. 3. Translation by J. W. Semple.

the principle governing their action toward each other should be that of good will.

A third principle immanent in the moral nature is the sacredness of personality. This is implied in both the absoluteness of moral obligation and the law of love. An obligation is absolute only when there is an absolute end to be achieved, and the law of love is absolutely binding only in case there are objects of intrinsic worth to be loved. In other words, it is only in the inviolable sanctity of personality that a rational basis can be found for the fundamental principles of the moral life. For apart from personality the moral life can have no self-sufficient end. "Every intelligent nature," and it only, "exists as an end in itself." From this Kant's well-known "practical imperative" naturally followed: "So act that humanity, both in thy own person and that of others, be used as an end in itself, and never as a mere mean."[7] It was this idea of the independent and intrinsic worth of personality that also lay back of the Kantian categorical imperative: "Act as if the maxim of thy will were to become, by thy adopting it, a universal law of nature."[8] That is, act, never from a selfish motive, but always with due recognition of the sacred rights of others. The sanctity of

[7] *Ibid.*, p. 42.
[8] *Ibid.*, p. 34.

personality and the unselfish will are thus the essential elements in the moral life in so far as the latter is categorically obligatory upon us. And these various factors, including the sense of obligation itself, are all a priori principles of the practical or moral reason.

There is a fourth subjective principle of the moral life which is not so commonly recognized nor so easily defined. It is the ideal of humanity.[9] We recognize it in the injunction to act like a man, to be a man, a true man. But the exact content of this ideal is not easily determined. It is a complex and with many a vague affair. We have a general sense of the direction in which it lies; but a precise analysis of it is beyond us. We concede to it a certain authority, but just why is not always clear. And yet the principle is one that has an important practical bearing on the moral life. It is not universal as is the law of good will, valid for all moral beings. It has to do with human perfection, an ideal relative to humanity. But as such an ideal it conditions the application of the law of love. The latter might be fulfilled among sots and gluttons. It becomes truly ethical only when it takes into account the human ideal of dignity and worth and is applied accordingly.

---

[9] Called by Edgar S. Brightman, "The Law of the Ideal of Personality." See his *Moral Laws,* pp. 242ff.

Such, then, is the moral equipment of mankind from the subjective standpoint: the distinction between right and wrong and the obligation to do the right and avoid the wrong, the law of good will, the sacredness of personality, and the ideal of humanity. These principles, to adopt Hume's putting of the case, are "founded on the original constitution of the mind,"[10] and without them an ethical vocabulary would never have arisen, and, if it had somehow been invented, would have conveyed no meaning. Our innate capacity for moral distinctions is the precondition of all moral experience; and this capacity is underived and self-validating.

A similar line of thought may also be developed with reference to the aesthetic nature. It too has its own categories and stands in its own right. But for our present purpose it is unnecessary that this truth should be elaborated. It is here sufficient that we recognize the fundamental parallel between the aesthetic nature and the moral and theoretical natures which we have briefly analyzed. Our immediate concern is with the religious nature and its relation to the other essential aspects of our being.

We speak of both the religious nature and the religious reason. Each term has its special connotation. But they may be used synonymously,

---

[10] *Inquiry Concerning Principles of Morals,* sect. V.

and it is in this sense that I shall for the most part employ them. According to Kant, there is a rational or a priori element in religion, but this element does not have the same specific character as the moral a priori. It is, rather, derived from the latter. The beliefs in God and immortality are, it is true, distinctively religious beliefs, and they are what Kant calls "synthetic judgments a priori"; that is, they are not analytic implications of other ideas nor are they given in experience. Nevertheless, they are not self-validating as is the categorical imperative. They are, rather, inferences drawn from the moral nature, postulates of the practical reason. Without God and without immortality the moral will would face an impossible task. This is evident from the fact that the *summum bonum* as the necessary goal of life contains two essential elements, personal holiness and the harmony of happiness with morality, and from the further fact that neither of these can be attained by mortal man. Holiness implies "a perfection of which no rational being of the sensible world is capable at any moment of his existence."[11] Its realization is an endless task, and so requires as its condition an endless life. On the other hand, an endless life would not effect the harmony of

[11] Kant's *Theory of Ethics*, p. 218. Translation by T. K. Abbott.

happiness with morality. For that an omnipotent Being is needed; and so the moral nature postulates the existence of God.

This derivation of religion from the practical or moral reason represented in certain respects an advance beyond the earlier theoretical arguments for the divine existence. But it never completely satisfied the religious mind. It did not allow religion to come fully to itself, to express itself in its own unique and distinctive character. It subordinated the religious to the moral nature, and failed to accord to the former the same self-verifying power that it claimed for the latter.

A reaction against this phase of the Kantian teaching, consequently, set in. Schleiermacher, with his rich religious nature and his Moravian training, insisted that religion is not a derivative from either morality or science. It is "neither a knowing nor a doing, but a modification of feeling or of immediate self-consciousness." "It is an affection, a revelation of the Infinite in the finite, God being seen in it and it in God." It is "the consciousness of being absolutely dependent, or, which is the same thing, of being in relation with God." It is thus "something different from a mixture of opinions . . . and precepts," something far deeper and more significant than "an instinct craving for a mess of metaphysical and ethical crumbs." It "takes its place alongside of science and practice as a necessary, an indispensable third, as their natural counterpart, not less in worth and splendor than either."[12]

As such a fundamental and independent phase of human consciousness religion has its own distinct nature. It represents a unique capacity of the human spirit and carries with it its own justification. Its essence, according to Schleiermacher, is to be found in the feeling of absolute dependence. This feeling, he tells us in words previously quoted, is "not an accidental element, nor a thing which varies from person to person, but is a universal element of life; and the recognition of this fact entirely takes the place, for the system of doctrine, of all so-called proofs of the existence of God."[13] In other words, religion finds its proof in itself, in its own universality and inevitability. There is in religious experience an "immediate certitude of God," and this certitude justifies itself. It requires no extraneous support, any more than does the corresponding certitude implicit in moral experience and sense experience. The self-certainty of religious experience takes the place of the Biblical, ecclesiastical, and rationalistic authorities of the past.

---

[12] *On Religion: Speeches to its Cultured Despisers,* translated by J. Oman, pp. 18, 31, 35f., 37f.

[13] *The Christian Faith,* paragraph 33.

In it we have a sufficient basis for Christian theology.

Such in the main was Schleiermacher's contention. He found in the religious nature of man a valid principle of self-verification. In this respect subsequent theology has to a large extent followed his lead. But the religious nature of man has been variously conceived. The predominant tendency, represented by Schleiermacher himself, has been anti-rationalistic or anti-intellectualistic. Religion has been interpreted largely in emotional or mystical and volitional or practical terms; and this interpretation has been quite generally accepted. There is, however, a peril in it. There is the danger of subjectivism or illusionism, the danger that religion will be robbed of its objective validity and reduced to a purely mystical or humanistic cult. Some have consequently felt the need of emphasizing the rational or intellectual element in religion. They speak of a religious reason as distinguished from the theoretical, the moral, and the aesthetic reason. There is, they tell us, a religious a priori, independent of and co-ordinate with the three other rational a prioris; and this a priori is constitutive of man's religious nature and the creative source of his religious experience.

The idea of a religious a priori is implicit, as we have seen, in the Kantian philosophy; but it is only comparatively recently that the term has come into use.[14] Its currency is due largely to the influence of Ernst Troeltsch (1865-1923), one of the most distinguished theologians and philosophers of religion of the past generation. The doctrine expressed by the term does not controvert the teaching of Schleiermacher with reference to the essentially emotional and practical character of religion. It recognizes the uniqueness of religious experience. But it does protest against a one-sided exaggeration of its uniqueness. It points to an underlying unity of the spiritual life. While religious experience differs from the three other fundamental forms of human experience, it is not opposed to them. It is, rather, akin to them. They are all grounded in a common human reason. They all have their source in principles immanent in the human mind. All are the expressions of a-priori capacities of the human spirit. They consequently tend to support each other. There is no civil war between them; rather is there a fundamental harmony. The religious a priori takes its place along side of the other a prioris as an integral factor in human reason or human nature.

---

[14] For a more extended account of religious apriorism, see my article on the subject in *Studies in Philosophy and Theology*, pp. 93-127, edited by E. C. Wilm.

The structure of the religious a priori does not admit of so precise an analysis as does that of the theoretical and moral a prioris. Troeltsch contents himself with pointing out that the religious a priori is "formal" as are the Kantian categories in general, that it is "unique," that it is "anti-intellectualic," and that it is autonomously valid. Its inner content he leaves vague and undefined. Rudolf Otto is somewhat more specific in that he distinguishes three different forms of the religious a priori: the rational, the irrational, and "the connection of the rational and the nonrational elements in religion, their inward and necessary union."[15] By the rational religious a priori he means that "original and underivable capacity of mind" which expresses itself in the gradually clarified conception of Deity as possessed of such attributes as absoluteness, personality, and goodness. By the irrational religious a priori he means that native endowment of the mind which makes possible the *numinous* experience, an immediate awareness of the divine. By the third form of the religious a priori he means that immanent mental principle which leads us to recognize a necessary connection between the numinous or religious, on the one hand, and the ethical or rational, on the other. It was to such a native religious conscience that

[15] *The Idea of the Holy,* pp. 116, 140.

Amos and the Old-Testament prophets in general appealed, and it is through man's possession of such a conscience that the gradual moralization of religion has been brought about. Of these three forms of the religious a priori the second and third are more distinctly religious than the first, but all three are manifestly involved in religious experience.

There is, of course, nothing fixed or final about any analysis of the religious reason. We make our analyses so as to conform with what we regard as the essential elements of religion. If we look upon faith as the essence of religion, we may with Paul Kalweit[16] say that faith is the religious a priori; and if in addition we regard certain mystical and ethical elements as essential to religion, we may treat them also as religious a prioris.[17] The important thing is to recognize that religion, whatever be its essential elements, has its rootage in the a priori or rational structure of the human mind.

---

[16] "Das Religiöse Apriori" in *Theologische Studien und Kritiken,* 1908, pp. 139-156.

[17] We might, for instance, speak of what James calls the "mystical germ" as a or the religious a priori. See J. S. Bixler, *Religion in the Philosophy of William James,* pp. 194f. James disclaimed having a mystical experience of his own, but "there is," he said, "a germ in me of something similar that makes admiring response." "Without any mystical germ in us," he wrote Leuba, "we would all unhesitatingly hold to a dogmatic atheistic naturalism.' "

Religious Apriorism

"Religious a priori" may not be an altogether happy phrase. The word "a priori" belongs primarily to logic, and hence has associations that may seem to unfit it as a designation or description of man's religious nature. But however that may be, the phrase does naturally suggest two fundamental and significant truths with respect to religion. The first is its original and underivable character; the second its autonomous validity. The first we have already emphasized; the second remains to be considered. But before passing to a consideration of this important truth or principle there are some preliminary explanations that should be made.

For one thing, it should be pointed out that the existence of a religious a priori, or a native religious capacity of the human mind, has no direct bearing on the psychological nature of religious experience. It does not favor one theory as over against another. It cannot be claimed as an ally by the emotionalist, the mystic, the moralist, the intellectualist, or even the eclectic who sees in religion a fusion of all the different factors emphasized in a one-sided way by the others. These psychological theories are all consistent with religious apriorism. Whatever religion may be from the psychological standpoint, it requires for its explanation an immanent mental principle, an a priori. There is nothing in the religious a priori that necessarily limits its expression to any one phase of our mental life, nor is there anything in it that necessarily extends it to our life as a whole. What the actual fact is must be determined by a study of the history and psychology of religion. If religion in its great historic forms has uniformly expressed itself in the various fundamental aspects of human experience, in feeling, willing, and thinking, we may naturally assume that this is its normal expression and that the religious a priori is a creative principle which is operative within the mind as a whole. There is no logical necessity that it should be so. But the facts clearly favor this view, and it is also what we would naturally expect in view of the profound character of the religious experience. We may then adopt it, but in doing so we need to bear in mind that it is not an implication of religious apriorism. The religious a priori is a presupposition of religious experience, regardless of the particular psychological content that we attribute to the experience.

There is also nothing in religious apriorism that enables us to decide the question as to whether religious experience is ultimately perceptual or inferential in its nature. The question, as we have already pointed out, is not so significant as is commonly supposed. The fact is that the perceptual type of experience is not necessarily any more trustworthy than the inferential. Indeed, there is at bottom no very sharp difference between them. In all perception there is more or less of inference, and in all inference there is more or less of perceptual activity. Take, for instance, the objective reference of thought. This is an essential element in perception; yet it is obviously inferential in character, even though it is a spontaneous act of the mind and so instantaneous as to be unobserved. What I, however, wish here to direct attention to is that the religious a priori may express itself as truly in an inferential as in a perceptual process. If man's instinctive quest after life leads him to infer the existence of a supreme and transcendent God and a supreme and transcendent Power, there is no reason why this inference should not be ascribed to the religious a priori in the same way that a numinous experience is. And if it could be shown that the numinous experience was originally developed by an inferential process out of more elementary emotions of wonder, awe, and fear, there is no reason why it should on that account be any less in need of the religious a priori for its explanation. The inferential theory of religious experience is quite as consistent with religious apriorism as is the perceptual theory.[18]

Another point worth noting is that religious apriorism conceives of the mind not as "a disinterested logic-machine," but as "a living organism with manifold interests and tendencies." These interests and tendencies express original capacities of the human mind, and in so far as they do so, are a priori. They underlie our mental activity as a whole—intellectual, moral, aesthetic, and religious; and in their fundamental and essential nature they constitute the ultimate standard and test of truth. If our profoundest interests and needs are satisfied by a belief, that belief may be accepted as true. This is the principle underlying pragmatism, and in that respect religious apriorism and religious pragmatism are at one. Apriorism acknowledges

[18] A distinction, however, needs to be made between "mediate" and "immediate" inference. The latter is implicit in religious perception and points to a native religious capacity in man. Mediate inference, on the other hand, is a deduction from religious experience. For instance, in a recent book by John Macmurray on *The Structure of Religious Experience* the idea of God is said to be "inherent in the act of religious reflection." It is not given immediately in religious experience. We infer the existence of God from the coexistence of finite selves. This inference, we are told, is logically inevitable. It cannot be rejected without self-contradiction. But it does not require a distinct religious a priori. It gives us a God who is "the primary correlate of human rationality" rather than the direct object of religious intuition.

the validity of the pragmatic appeal to the values of religious experience, to its inner joys and its beneficial consequences. These values are satisfactions of our religious needs and interests, and as such are within certain limits valid evidence of the truth of religion. The difference between apriorism and pragmatism lies in the fact that the former grounds this conviction in the structure of the human mind, in its a priori capacities, in a way that pragmatism with its empiricistic leanings is unable to do. Apriorism does not, then, reject the pragmatic method in religious argumentation. It accepts and utilizes it, but at the same time supplements it in a significant way by providing it with a more substantial philosophical underpinning. Religious pragmatism is true so far as it goes, but it does not go far enough.

Still another point to be observed is that the evidence for the existence of a religious a priori is to be found primarily, not in an analysis of the individual mind, but in the history of the race. It is the universality and apparent inevitability of religion that leads us to believe that it is structural in human nature or the human reason. The religious experiences of a relatively few favored individuals may be more striking and interesting than those of people in general, but they are not so significant. The most impressive thing about religion is not its extraordinary manifestations in the lives of a few, but the common religious faith of the masses of mankind as this is expressed in the great religions of the world. Here we have to do with a great racial fact—a fact that is manifestly grounded in human nature itself. The unique religious experiences of unusual individuals might conceivably be chance variations without further significance. But not so the faith of men in general. It points to a common human capacity, to a true religious a priori. Only on this assumption can the universality of religion be accounted for.

One further truth with respect to the religious a priori should be noted. This has to do with its motive—a motive analogous to that of Kantian apriorism in general. What Kant sought to do was to save reason and the cultural interests of mankind from the disintegrating influence of the sensationalistic and empiricistic philosophy. This was his primary aim, but it was not his only aim. He wanted to save reason, not only from skepticism, but also from the cramping influence of the dogmatisms of the past. It was this double purpose that led him to create the "critical philosophy" with its theoretical and practical a prioris. He showed, as we have seen, that there are principles immanent in the mind, which no psychology can dissolve away, and which are essential in order to make not only psychology but even experience itself possible. We are, therefore, warranted in retaining our faith in reason. But while there are rational or a priori principles underlying experience, these principles, according to Kant, do not enable us to go beyond experience; and hence he concluded that there is no theoretical basis for the traditional metaphysical beliefs. The latter are justifiable only in so far as they serve the purposes of the practical reason. They have no independent validity that saves them from criticism. So reason with its aprioristic principles stands in its own right as over against empiricistic skepticism, on the one hand, and an uncritical dogmatism, on the other.

What Kant thus sought to do for reason as a whole, especially for the sciences and morality, the modern advocate of religious apriorism seeks to do for religion. Religion is today confronted with a double danger. On the one hand, there are the various psychological and sociological attempts to explain religion as an illusion.[19] It is said to be the baseless product of fear, of dreams and trances, of the personifying tendency of the human mind, of prescientific modes of thought, of the objectification of desire, of unjust social conditions, of perverted sexuality, and of other

[19] See my *Doctrine of God,* pp. 20-38.

unworthy and misleading causes. It has thus no rational justification and is destined to disappear with the progress of science. This is the conclusion to which a naturalistic philosophy logically leads. On the other hand, as over against this tendency in modern thought we have Barthianism and the various traditional theologies which appeal to some absolute authority of the past and deny to reason the right of invading the sacred precincts of faith. The result is a failure of religion to adjust itself to modern modes of thought, and an exposure of itself to a devastating criticism.

To meet this double peril, one coming from theological irrationalism and the other from philosophical naturalism, a philosophy is needed which makes it clear that religion is something wrought into the very texture of human reason, that it is not a transitory or illusory phase of the social life of man but is woven into the very warp and woof of the human mind, so that it stands in its own right and is a permanent and essential constituent of human nature. Such a philosophy the doctrine of a religious a priori seeks to present. It contends for the rationality and inevitability of faith, and in doing so carries on a twofold polemic. One is directed against a destructive relativism and the other against a blind authoritarianism. As against these two tendencies in modern thought the religious apriorist maintains that religion is grounded as deeply and ineradicably in the human spirit as are science, morality, and art.

Autonomous Validity

We come now to the most significant aspect of religious apriorism, an aspect to which we have already referred. This is its teaching with reference to the autonomous validity of religion. All that has thus far been said about the religious a priori has been preliminary. We have sought to explain the doctrine in a general way, to point out some of its implications, and to set forth the type of philosophy out of which it emerged. This has been necessary as a kind of propaedeutic. Without some insight into the philosophy of Kant and the theology of Schleiermacher it would be difficult to understand the doctrine fully, and difficult also to appreciate how deeply it is grounded in the main stream of modern thought. It has its rootage in the great idealistic movement of the past century, and apart from this connection is likely to be misunderstood and to lose its appealing power.

It is not, however, the history of the doctrine, nor its philosophical background, nor its psychological implications, with which we are here especially concerned, but its apologetic significance. That the religious a priori denotes an original and underived capacity of the human spirit, that it is "formal" in the Kantian sense of the term, that it is not intellectualistic, that it is a creative principle underlying the religious life as a whole, that it is psychologically neutral, that it guarantees the permanence of religious experience—all these are interesting and valuable items of information. But they derive their interest and value chiefly from the fact that they prepare the way for the view that the religious a priori is not dependent on anything outside itself for its validity. It is an autonomous validity, a self-verifying aspect of our mental life.

The ultimate basis of this principle of self-verification is to be found in the metaphysical reality of the mind, in its creative activity, and in the fact that its activities result in certain fundamental and irreducible types of experience such as the sensuous or scientific, the ethical, the aesthetic, and the religious. These different types of experience represent distinct capacities and basic interests and tendencies of the human mind. They are not created nor are they validated by formal logic. They validate themselves in the sense that they and their implications or postulates may be accepted as valid, if they do not contradict the laws of reason. This is the mode of procedure actually adopted by the human mind when not debauched by formal logic. Bowne has formulated the law as simply and convincingly as anyone. "Whatever," he says, "the mind demands for the satisfaction of its subjective interests and tendencies may be assumed as real in default of positive disproof."[20]

This is the law which we follow in the natural sciences. We assume the intelligibility of the world and our ability to understand it, and then proceed to interpret our sense experiences as best we can. That the world is intelligible and that we are able to understand it cannot be demonstrated. But there is no positive disproof of it. So we assume it, and on the basis of this assumption or faith build up our natural sciences. The irrationality of nature and its uninterpretability are quite possible conceptions. They do not violate the formal laws of thought. But they do run counter to the basal interests and needs of our nature. If we were to accept them, life would be crippled, thought would have no object, and action no aim. We, consequently, reject them, not because they are theoretically impossible, but because they are practically absurd. Life with us has the right of way, and whatever satisfies our deepest interests and needs commends itself to us as true. Our intellectual interest in truth requires us to believe in the

---

[20] *Theism*, p. 18.

rationality of the world and in our ability to understand it. Hence we adopt this belief without serious question and make it the basis of our science and our philosophy. To some extent we confirm its truth by observation, experimentation, and reflection; but this does not carry us very far. No demonstration of its truth is possible. In the last analysis the belief in the intelligibility of the world remains a belief. All theoretical knowledge rests on faith.

It is so also with our religious nature or interest. It expresses itself in faith in a supersensible and divine order; and on the basis of this faith we construct our theologies. Our religious knowledge is founded on faith in the same way that our scientific and philosophic knowledge is. The faith is different in the two cases. But it is faith in one instance as truly as in the other, and logically one type of faith is as valid as the other. There is no a priori reason why scientific faith should be accepted and religious faith rejected. These two represent fundamental interests of the human spirit; and if we accept the validity of one, the logical and reasonable thing is to accept the validity of the other. Religion has thus as firm a basis as has science. It justifies itself. This insight has profound significance. It gives to religious experience an impregnable position and, in my opinion, is the only adequate foundation for an empirical apologetic.

In ascribing to religious experience this self-verifying power we are, of course, not claiming for it infallibility. All experience is subject to criticism. This is as true of religious experience as it is of sense experience, of moral experience, and of aesthetic experience. Every mode of experience is fallible and may lead us astray. But if we are not to fall into complete skepticism, we must hold to the essential trustworthiness of the human mind, and we must attribute this trustworthiness, not to the theoretical reason alone, but to the whole mind. There is no rational warrant for accepting one of the three or four fundamental aspects of our mental life and rejecting the others. If the theoretical reason is trustworthy, this fact itself is presumptive evidence that the religious reason is also trustworthy. If, on the other hand, the latter is untrustworthy, the probability is that the former is such also. For the mind is a unit; and since it is such, we are justified in assuming that what it does along one fundamental line is as valid as what it does along another and parallel line. One phase of its activity supports the other. The theoretical and religious reasons stand or fall together.

But it is only essential truthfulness that we

can claim for either. Both of them may and do err. They need criticism and guidance. This, of course, also holds true of our moral and aesthetic natures. The mind as a whole is subject to error, and can escape it only through constant self-criticism. In all the fundamental forms of its activity it has a capacity for truth, but it does not and cannot attain the truth automatically. It must deliberately and critically seek the truth in order to find it.

In this process of self-criticism it is implied that there are standards or norms of truth; and it is further implied that these norms are to be found within the mind itself. While the mind is not automatic, it is autonomous. It has its own laws, the norms of its own activity, within itself. This is true of the practical as well as the theoretical reason. There is a normative principle in religion, in morality, and in art, as there is in science and philosophy. Just how these norms arise we do not know. But they are implicit in reason itself, and we must recognize them. We must distinguish the logical from the psychological, the normative from the factual. If we did not do so, truth itself would vanish. Norms are the presupposition of all quest after truth and of all high spiritual endeavor.

To recognize and define these norms, however, is no easy task, especially in the practical field.

Here about all that we can do is to acquaint ourselves with the various cultural developments of human history, compare them with each other, reflect on them, live ourselves into them, and then wait for the response of our own spirit as to what is normative and valid. The decision in each case must rest with the mind itself. There is no extramental standard either in religion or morality or art. In all these fields the mind is autonomous. It has its own a priori; and each of these a prioris is normative. It carries within itself its own standard, its own principle of self-criticism.

This standard or principle, however, is not in the nature of an innate idea. Its concrete content cannot be determined by psychological analysis. What its essential nature is can be learned only from history. And here the standards we discover are not and cannot be absolute. They point forward to and approximate the ideal goal rather than realize it. This is as true in religion as elsewhere. We learn what is essential and normative in the religious nature of man only by a critical study of the religions of the world. Here we have revealed to us the concrete products of the religious a priori. These products vary in character. Many are peculiar to the individual and manifestly nonessential. But along with them are the great catholic sentiments and beliefs of the race. These have been built up through the centuries. They have passed through the fires of criticism. They represent "the survival of the fittest." If the essential and normative nature of religion is to be found anywhere, it certainly must be in these fundamental and universal elements in religious experience. It is these elements that express the true religious a priori and that stand in their own right.

Bowne used to emphasize the fact that these basal catholic beliefs of humanity are superindividual, that they are made for us rather than by us, and from this used to conclude that they have "the significance of any other great natural product. They show the direction of the evolving movement, the trend of the universe of mind. They are no longer accidents of the individual, but are as much entitled to be viewed as belonging to the nature of things as the stars in their courses or the law of gravitation."[21] In this line of thought there is profound truth. A theistic evolutionist could hardly view the developing religious life and beliefs of mankind otherwise. He would naturally find in them an expression of the divine reason. But this does not bring us to the root of the matter. What Bowne says

[21] "Faith in Our Immortality" in *The Independent,* 48 (1896), p. 439. Quoted by E. T. Ramsdell in *The Personalist,* 1935, p. 32f.

on this subject is really only a supplement to the doctrine of man's creation. If man is made in the image of God, we may obviously trust his faculties, and we may trust them all the more confidently as they approach a greater and greater degree of maturity. It is this fact that gives such profound significance to the great catholic beliefs and tendencies of humanity. "Their universality and necessity are the best of grounds for belief;"[22] and they are such because through their universality and necessity we see that these beliefs and tendencies are rooted in the essential nature of man. This nature we must trust in the religious field as well as elsewhere, if we are not to be engulfed in complete skepticism. A logical basis for this trust may be found in a theistic world view; but whether we find it there or not, the trust itself is necessary if the whole system of knowledge is not to be involved in disaster.

It is, then, in the religious nature of man, in the religious a priori, that religious experience finds its justification. It validates itself. But it does so only to him who has religion, who knows by his own experience what a vital and essential thing religion is in a full-orbed human life. And to such a person it is evident that the more vivid and vigorous one's religious experience is, the stronger and more trustworthy is the assurance

[22] B. P. Bowne, *Theory of Thought and Knowledge,* p. 377.

that accompanies it. Abraham Lincoln once said, "I do not believe in the American people, but I do believe in the American people aroused." One might also say the same of religion: "I do not believe in the religious nature of man, but I do believe in the religious nature of man aroused." It is an aroused religious experience, an experience which is earnest and vital, that carries assurance and conviction with it and that impresses the world with its sincerity.

The situation is analogous in the intellectual and moral realms. It is an awakened intellect and an awakened conscience that is the guide to truth and the norm of truth. There is no absolute immediacy in objective experience anywhere that guarantees its truth; nor does the inspirational value of any doctrine prove its objective validity. The sole basis of certainty is to be found in the mind itself. It is a quickened and enlightened intellect, a quickened and enlightened conscience, and a quickened and enlightened religious nature that constitute the only valid ground of certainty in these different fields. Error, illusion, and fanaticism are possible everywhere. There is no complete protection against them. But despite this fact we have an instinctive confidence in the essential trustworthiness of our own nature. On this confidence our whole intellectual and spiritual life is founded. We trust our profoundest insights; and this trust is as fully warranted in religion as elsewhere. On it as a basis we make our fundamental religious affirmations; and we do so with as much confidence and as good a conscience as we make similar affirmations in the field of science and philosophy.

William James used to say half humorously that he was "a better Methodist" than Borden P. Bowne. This Bowne would never admit. For one of the most characteristic features of the Methodist movement has been its note of assurance, and this we find in Bowne to a far greater degree than in James. Both men agreed with Wesley in his emphasis on religious experience. Both made experience basal in their philosophy of religion. But James confined himself for the most part to surface phenomena. He operated with pragmatic considerations and with mystical immediacy as though they were finalities. Now and then he recognized that they needed further justification, but his philosophy did not permit him to accept an aprioristic theory of the mind, and so he resorted to what Otto calls "somewhat singular and mysterious hypotheses."[23] These hypotheses may have some value, but they do not go deep enough to justify a profound and vigorous type of religious assurance.

---

[23] *The Idea of the Holy,* p. 11.

Bowne, on the other hand, with his Kantian background, went beneath the surface of religious experience and found its source in the structure of the mind itself. There is in man, as he maintained, a religious nature or a religious reason, as fundamental, independent, and trustworthy as is the theoretical reason itself. This rational religious nature is the presupposition of religious experience. It is an ultimate fact of our mental life and justifies itself. We are, therefore, warranted in reposing as much confidence in the reasoned conclusions of religious experience as in the corresponding conclusions of our sensuous, moral, and aesthetic experience. Indeed, from its own, if not from the logical, point of view, religious experience may claim for itself an even higher degree of certainty. For as religious people we believe that our experience of God is not simply our own achievement, it is "a gift of God." In the great affirmations of faith the Divine Spirit witnesseth with our spirit. A double witness thus attests their truth. The divine witness, it is true, transcends our philosophy. But there is nothing in the principle of self-verification that excludes it. Rather does the self-verifying power of religious experience lead by its very nature to that highest form of assurance which regards itself as born of the Spirit of God.

CHAPTER V

CHRISTIAN EXPERIENCE

In the preceding chapters we have considered the validity of religious experience in general. Our main contention has been that the ultimate basis for the belief in the validity of religious experience is to be found, not in its immediacy nor in its practical utility, but in the native religious endowment of the human spirit, an endowment that is as fundamental, independent, and trustworthy as is our native capacity for sense experience, moral experience, and aesthetic experience. Religion, we have argued, is structural in the human mind, and as such has logically as valid a basis as has philosophy or morality or art. These fundamental interests of the human spirit all stand in their own right. One is not the source of any of the others. Each is an autonomous validity. It verifies itself. No profounder validation of our basic beliefs is possible.

From the philosophical grounding of religious experience as a whole we now turn to Christian experience and the question of its validity. Essentially the same line of argumentation applies here also. We appeal to the religious nature of man to justify not only the general truths of religion but also the special truths of the Christian faith. There is, therefore, no fundamental cleavage between Christianity and other religions. They all consciously or unconsciously appeal for their validation to the common religious reason. The difference between them is a difference of degree. On this difference of degree is to be based the Christian claim to a special divine revelation and to a unique authority. The Christian type of experience professes to be the purest and most highly developed form of religious experience, and in so far as this is true it is warranted in claiming for itself a larger degree of validity than any other kind of religious life or belief. It does not deny all truth to other religious systems. It acknowledges that there is a light that lighteth every man that cometh into the world. If there were no such light, if there were no native insight into religious truth, there would be nothing in men that would enable them to receive and appropriate the "revealed" truth of the Christian faith. Christian experience presupposes the common religious experience of mankind and is built upon it.

It is sometimes said that we may concede partial truth to the ethnic faiths only in case we first believe in Christ. Only on the assumption that Christianity is true can we attribute any truth to other religions. The reason given is this: If religion in its highest or Christian form is not true, it is obvious that we cannot ascribe even partial truth to religion in its lower forms. If the light that is in Christianity is darkness, this must be still more true of other religions. The latter are valid only in so far as they are forerunners of a valid Christian faith. It is their relationship to Christianity that gives to them whatever validity they have. In this line of reasoning there is obviously some truth. But, on the other hand, it is also true that man's native capacity for religious faith, as revealed in other religions, is the necessary presupposition of our appreciation of the Christian faith. Christ would mean nothing to us unless there were already within us a native yearning after the divine. It is quite as true that the common religious experience of men makes possible and validates Christian experience, as it is that Christian experience gives partial validation to our common religious experience. The strict fact, however, is that neither type of religious experience validates the other. Both find their justification in the essential trustworthiness of man's religious nature. It is man's religious a priori or native capacity for God that warrants our accepting both the validity of religious experience in general and the unique claims of the Christian faith.

The Uniqueness of Christian Experience

To this type of Christian apologetic considerable objection is at present being raised. It is objected, first, that Christian experience differs not only in degree but also in kind from all other types of religious experience. In the next place, it is objected that the theory in question attributes Christian experience to a human capacity instead of the Divine Spirit, and hence runs counter to New-Testament teaching. It is still further objected that the theory renders impossible the absolute certainty which Christian faith demands. These three objections stand closely related to each other. They all owe their origin to a mistaken supernaturalism, and to a dualistic view of human history. But while they have this common source, they are sufficiently distinct to be treated separately.

The idea that there is a radical difference of kind between Christian and non-Christian experience goes back to the early Church. It was then the common belief that Biblical religion was true and that all other religions were false. Occasionally a more generous attitude toward the latter was expressed, but for the most part the posture was one of irreconcilable antagonism. The gods of the heathen were "no gods," they were "evil spirits." To worship them had no truth or virtue in it. The whole structure of heathen worship was regarded as belonging to the realm of darkness. It had either a diabolic or a purely human source.

This intransigent attitude toward other religions no doubt had a temporary value. It saved the apostles and early Christian missionaries from the danger of compromising with heathen beliefs and practices, and at the same time it gave them an heroic zeal they probably would not otherwise have had. They were seeking to introduce into the world a higher conception of God and a purer standard of conduct; and this they were able to do all the more effectively because they regarded the new life and the new faith as the very antithesis of the life and faith which they were trying to supplant. This antithesis was in part theoretical, an outgrowth of the uncritical philosophy of history current in the early Church. But it was not wholly such. To most of the early Christians it seemed justified by the actual differences between the new and the old faiths.

But at present to draw so sharp a line between Christian experience and all other forms of religious experience would to most of us seem unwarranted. The facts are against it. In the religious consciousness, as revealed to us by the psychology and the history of religion, there is an underlying unity. Theologies and mythologies may differ in multifarious ways, but in the subjective experience itself, in the mental attitude of the worshiper, there is an observable identity. Prayer is much the same among the most diverse races and individuals.

Then, too, modern thought is dominated by the ideas of evolution and of continuity. All history, we are told, is of one weave. There is no place in it for such a fundamental contrast as is involved in the traditional conception of the distinction between Christianity and other religions. This theory, it is true, may not be wholly justified either by the facts or by speculation. But there can be no doubt that the current conviction with reference to the essential unity of history is so strong that it cannot be disregarded, if we are successfully to commend Christianity to the modern mind. We must think of the Christian faith as organically related to other faiths. Our modern philosophy of the divine immanence forbids such a sharp antithesis between the Christian and the non-Christian world as was current in the early and medieval Church and as has in recent years been reaffirmed in the Barthian theology.

The philosophy of immanence also excludes the antithetical relation of the human to the divine, which underlies the second objection above referred to.[1] According to this objection the theory of a religious a priori or of a native religious capacity in man is out of harmony with the New-Testament teaching that faith is the gift of God. If faith comes from God, man can have no part in its production. What man does belongs to the natural order, and hence is excluded from the sphere of the divine activity. The divine is unnatural, and the natural is undivine. This is a common assumption in popular religious thought. It is also a basic element in the Barthian theology.

The assumption, however, has no philosophical warrant. Man's capacity for God is God-given; and since it is such, there is no reason why it should be regarded as a rival of the Divine Spirit or as in any sense exclusive of it. A capacity that comes from God cannot be made a valid ground of human pride, nor can it properly become a barrier between man and God. Rather is it a necessary presupposition of any real union between the human and the divine. Without it faith could not even be received as a divine gift. If we are to exercise faith, it is obvious that we must have the capacity to exercise it. Faith can become ours only in so far as we ourselves believe. Only by believing can we receive

[1] See Borden P. Bowne, *The Immanence of God,* and Francis J. McConnell, *The Diviner Immanence.*

the faith that God gives us. Our ability to believe, our capacity for God, in no way excludes, it, rather, presupposes, our dependence upon him. It assumes the divine initiative rather than the reverse. There is, therefore, no conflict between the theory of a religious a priori and the New-Testament doctrine of the divine grace. The latter is based, not on a metaphysical dualism, but on the relation of dependence in which we necessarily stand to the Creator.

The third objection to the aprioristic theory of Christian experience has to do, as above stated, with the problem of certainty. It is argued that the Christian faith requires and implies absolute assurance, and that such assurance is impossible unless there be an infallible standard or source of Christian experience which differentiates the latter from all other forms of religious experience. In the past this condition was met by the doctrine of Biblical or ecclesiastical infallibility. The Bible or the Church was regarded as possessed of divine authority. But whatever practical value this doctrine may have had, its validity was always open to question, and any assurance that may have been gained from it must have been in the nature of formal assent rather than a living conviction. In any case that type of authority has lost its influence with the modern mind.

A new authoritarianism, however, which seeks to accomplish essentially the same purpose, has of late arisen under the leadership of Karl Barth. Barth and his associates repudiate all reliance on "the treacherous snow bridges of mystical experience" and on any form of human effort or capacity. Our only ground of confidence, they tell us, is God. But God does not manifest himself in the stream of human consciousness or of human history. His Word is not to be identified with any book or institution. His existence is in the strictest sense of the word superempirical. We do not and cannot know him at first hand or through any quest of our own. Only through an act of faith can we lay hold of him. And this act can be wrought within us only by the Divine Spirit. We cannot through any volition of our own exercise saving faith. Nor can we even know that such faith has been divinely wrought within us. We can only "believe that we believe."

If this be actually the case, Christian assurance, as ordinarily understood, would seem to be excluded rather than rationally or authoritatively grounded. The only assurance possible on such a basis would be of a speculative nature. It would rest on the doctrine of election. We may, for instance, have the theological conviction that God will certainly save those whom he purposes to save. The elect will certainly be redeemed. But who the elect are, we do not and cannot know. We may by a process of self-hypnotism persuade ourselves that we belong to the number.[2] But this conclusion would manifestly have no rational warrant. It might be true, but it might be wholly illusory. The abstract doctrine of predestination does not guarantee the election of any particular person, nor does it validate his religious convictions. It leaves the problem of Christian assurance in as great uncertainty as ever. Indeed, it accentuates the uncertainty.

The fact is that absolute certainty in religious belief is a theological will-o'-the-wisp. The quest after it has time and again led men astray. They have sought it in infallible standards of truth, in the immediacy of religious experience, in its assumed divine source, and in its supreme worth. But all of these are open to question. No indubitable certainty is here possible. All certainty and all knowledge, as we have repeatedly stated, is ultimately based on faith, faith in the essential trustworthiness of our faculties. If our religious faculty or nature is trustworthy, we

[2] This is what the older Calvinists did. It was this fact that made them such a power in Europe. Not a few Communists today derive a similar courage and confidence from their "dialectical materialism." See B. H. Streeter, *The God Who Speaks,* pp. 7ff.

may repose a reasonable degree of confidence in the conclusions at which it has arrived through the long course of human history. These conclusions are not infallible. They have been arrived at through criticism, and are subject to criticism. But in so far as they meet the demands of the religious reason we may trust them; and the more completely they meet these demands, the greater will be our confidence in them. It is on this basis that we rest the unique claims of Christian experience. Christianity does not stand apart from all other religions as alone divine. It is not an island separated from the great human mainland. It is, rather, a mountainpeak rising up out of the broad plane of human need and human aspiration. It is the climax of the natural, not its antithesis. And in so far as it is such, in so far as it expresses and satisfies the deepest and highest needs of the human spirit, it may without hesitancy be accepted as valid. This is the method actually followed in validating our fundamental beliefs in general; and no other method is either possible or necessary in dealing with the Christian faith.

We do not exempt Christian experience from criticism. We subject it to the same tests that we do other forms of religious experience. Only by meeting these tests more adequately than other religions can Christianity properly claim the primacy over them. There is no exclusive divinity in Christian experience, which puts upon it the stamp of truth. Nor can its validity and its uniqueness be established by an appeal to authority or by a one-sided appeal to emotion or to practical consequences. The validation of Christian belief as of religious belief in general is a complex process and calls for the exercise of all the resources of the human mind, rational as well as empirical, intellectual as well as moral and emotional. No wholesale or short-cut method will suffice.

Our present concern, however, is not so much with the proper method of validating Christian experience, as with its theological interpretation. The chief barriers to belief lie in misunderstanding rather than hostile criticism. Especially is this true in a day when religious thought is seriously confused by conflicting currents. At such a time explanation is usually the best apologetic. What is most needed is a correct statement of what is involved in the Christian faith. To this task we shall now apply ourselves. We shall single out those elements in Christian experience that are theologically most significant, and expound their essential meaning. But before entering upon this task a brief word should be added with reference to the uniqueness of Christian experience.

First to be noted is the Christian's relationship to Jesus Christ. This relationship may be and is differently conceived. But whatever may be our theory of it, Christian experience is colored by the fact of Christ. It would not be truly Christian, if it were not. In some sense or other our Christian experience is mediated through him. We are his disciples. He is our Lord and Master. We have learned from him what God is, what man is, and what the way of life is, so that our religious experience is necessarily bound up with him. For us as Christians his being stands uniquely related to Deity.

But it is not simply a vague personal coloring that Jesus gives to Christian experience. He represents very definitely one of the two main types of religious experience that have appeared in the course of human history. These types have been called, respectively, the "prophetic" and the "mystical."[3] The latter in its more extreme form is represented by the religions of India and Neoplatonism in the Graeco-Roman world. The prophetic type appears in Zoroastrianism, Mosaism, Mohammedanism, and preeminently in Christianity. It stands for a personal as opposed to an impersonal view of Deity,

[3] Friedrich Heiler, *Das Gebet,* pp. 248-283. English translation, pp. 135-171. A. C. Knudson, *The Doctrine of God,* pp. 54-60.

for an optimistic as opposed to a pessimistic conception of the world, and for an ethical as opposed to an ecstatic ideal of the religious life. These points of distinction between prophetism and mysticism are, of course, not absolute. The two types of religious experience to some extent overlap each other. But in its main drift the prophetic type is personal, optimistic, and ethical, while the mystical type is impersonal, pessimistic, and ecstatic.

In its Christian form the prophetic type of religious experience has manifested itself in a deep consciousness of sin, a profound belief in the divine grace, and a strong spirit of hope.[4] These elements appear also in the other prophetic religions, but they have received in Christianity a unique development so that they may be regarded as characteristic aspects of Christian experience. They and the sense of personal relationship to Christ do not make up the total framework of the Christian life, but they are basic elements in it, and have doctrinal implications that make them especially significant for our present purpose. Each will be briefly considered. We begin with the consciousness of sin.

---

[4] Love or the ethical aspect of Christian experience is not here singled out for special consideration because there is at present no serious question as to its theological implications.

The Consciousness of Sin

All religion is rooted in human need. It is need that drives men to God and leads them to seek his aid. But need varies in kind. There is natural need, the need of food, shelter and other material and personal goods. With these needs religion was at first chiefly concerned, and it never becomes wholly indifferent to them. But religious need is never identical with natural need. It has its own unique satisfactions. The goods sought from God may be material or natural goods, but when received from him they cease to be merely material or natural and become sacramental. They become symbols of the divine presence and the divine favor. In other words, the religious relation is a more or less personal relation, a relation to Deity, and in this respect has a distinct quality of its own. Barth is mistaken when he says that "the religious impulse differs from the need of sleep only in degree."[5] There is a difference of kind between physical and religious need. There always has been. But in early times the relationship between them was closer than at present; religious satisfactions were more intimately intertwined with physical satisfactions.

The separation between them came about

[5] *Roemerbrief*, p. 219.

gradually. The spiritual detached itself more and more from the material until finally the soul and its needs became the primary objects of religious concern. The temporal and relative standpoint of earlier times was overcome. Religion centered its attention on the absolute and the eternal. It sought not simply relief from the temporal evils of life, but triumph over death itself. It was this absoluteness of the religious quest that now gave to religion its unique character. Indeed, it is doubtful if religion could have maintained itself in the world if it had not adopted the absolute standpoint, the standpoint of eternity. It is here that the very genius of the Christian faith and of all truly spiritual religion is to be found. Christianity is an absolute religion, a religion that meets an absolute need of the human spirit and that promises an ultimate absolute satisfaction.

It is, however, not only human mortality that creates the consciousness of an absolute need. The sense of our utter dependence upon a Higher Power is also awakened by our moral unworthiness. We seek holiness of life as well as immortality, and the former seems as far beyond the reach of our own strength as the latter. Man is not only mortal, he is a sinner and is unable to save himself. This is a fundamental note of Christian experience and an essential element in the Christian world view. Redemption comes from God and from him alone. Man can do nothing to merit it for himself. He is entirely dependent upon the divine grace. The Christian life is a life wholly derived from God, and its basal sentiment is the feeling of absolute dependence. In our own strength we can accomplish nothing. We are sinners, and all that is good within us we as Christians spontaneously acknowledge to be a gift of God.

That this is a correct description of one phase, and that an important phase, of valid Christian experience, would probably be generally admitted. After we have done all that we can, we are still, according to Jesus, to account ourselves "unprofitable servants." There is no just ground of religious pride in anything that we do. This thought appears again and again in our creeds and prayers, and manifestly expresses a genuine and profound Christian sentiment.

But what does it imply with reference to human nature? Does it assume that man is inherently evil? Does it mean that the human will is wholly impotent, that man is an utterly helpless being, and that God is so completely all in all that we have no real independence?

These questions introduce us to one of the great cleavages in Christian thought and, indeed, in religious thought in general. Among the

Ramanujas in India, for instance, there are two sharply divided schools of theology, one holding to what is called the "cat-hold theory" and the other to the "monkey doctrine."[6] According to the former, a man has no more to do with his own salvation than a helpless kitten which is seized by the nape of its neck and carried out of danger by its mother. According to the latter, man is like a baby monkey, which when carried to a place of safety by its mother hangs on with all the strength of its little arms. These two doctrines correspond to Calvinism and Arminianism in Protestant Christianity and to Augustinianism and Pelagianism or Semi-Pelagianism in Catholic Christianity.

The facts of Christian experience to which these divergent doctrines appeal are substantially the same. The Calvinist and the Arminian do not differ to any marked extent in their religious experiences. Both have toward God a feeling of trustful dependence and both have a sense of individual responsibility. The difference between them lies in their interpretation of these facts. According to the Calvinist, the dependence on God which we feel is absolute and excludes any real or metaphysical freedom on our part. Our sense of responsibility is secondary, and in so far as it seems to involve real

[6] George F. Moore, *History of Religions,* I., p. 337.

freedom, is illusory. Or if not, it is incapable of being reconciled with the profounder feeling of our dependence; in which case there is a fundamental antinomy in our thinking.

According to the Arminian, on the other hand, our dependence on God does not exclude a measure of independence. We owe, it is true, our redemption as well as our creation to God. We did not make ourselves nor can we remake ourselves. But we can and must supply the conditions under which the Divine Spirit can remake us. In other words, we have a limited power of contrary choice. On this power the Arminian bases both moral responsibility and the possibility of moral redemption. Without the power of alternativity there would be no truly moral life. But this power does not enable us to earn salvation for ourselves. Salvation is a divine gift. It is wholly dependent upon the divine grace. This is Christian teaching, both Arminian and Calvinistic.

There is, then, no dispute as to the feeling of dependence on God. It is basal in Christian experience. There is also no dispute as to the consciousness of sin. It too is a fundamental element in Christian experience. In the abstract there may be a question as to whether sin is absolutely universal. Theoretically it may be, and I believe is, possible that a responsible human being here and there may have lived for some time wholly free from sin. But for all practical purposes this possibility may be disregarded. "All have sinned, and come short of the glory of God." This Pauline word finds an echo in virtually every Christian heart. It expresses a profound Christian conviction, and is a presupposition of the Christian doctrine of redemption. Redemption in Christian thought is primarily redemption from sin. It means also ultimate redemption from suffering and death. But redemption from natural evil is from the Christian point of view secondary. Moral redemption comes first, and it implies a state of sin from which we are to be redeemed.

But how is the state of sin to be conceived? Is it to be regarded as the result of voluntary acts or as a condition inherent in our finitude or in the present structure of our being? Are we sinners by virtue of the fact that we are human, and are we on that account under the divine condemnation? Or are we sinners only in so far as we have actually done that which is evil in the divine sight? To these questions the answer of Christian experience is not altogether free from ambiguity. We judge ourselves from the standpoint of the ideal as well as from the standpoint of merit and demerit. From the standpoint of the ideal we feel ourselves utterly condemned. We are all "miserable sinners," sinful by nature, "dead in sin," and wholly unable to do anything ourselves to merit the divine favor. Everything good within us is the gift of the divine grace. Such is our feeling in prayer, as we stand face to face with the ideal. We are all Calvinists when we pray.

But however natural this emotional attitude toward Deity is, it is only one phase of Christian experience. We are dependent beings, but we are also responsible beings. We are summoned to obey the divine will, and exhorted to believe in the divine grace; and the assumption is that both the belief and the obedience are acts that lie within the range of our capacity. In believing and obeying we may be aided by the Divine Spirit, but the acts are nevertheless our own; and as such they point to a different conception of human nature from that which we have just described. We are not so totally sinful as to be devoid of any capacity for good. Merit as well as demerit, when properly understood, has its place in the ethical vocabulary of the Christian.[7]

[7] Wesley often became impatient with those who were "so dreadfully afraid of the word 'merit,'" and who nevertheless spoke of being rewarded "as our works deserved." Between these two expressions he could see no difference. "I cannot," he said, "split this hair. Whoever can has my leave. And afterward let him split his throat with crying out, 'O dreadful heresy.'" *Letters,* V., pp. 264f.

The extraordinary confusion which has appeared at this point in Christian thought, and which still prevails, has been due largely to a failure to distinguish the language of emotion from that of theology. In the presence of the greatness and holiness of God we inevitably feel our own littleness and sinfulness, and we feel them so keenly that we naturally express ourselves in unlimited terms of self-abasement. But this does not mean that we actually regard ourselves as totally depraved and wholly devoid of the power of contrary choice. Such an extreme view may be suggested by the language that we employ in prayer. But it runs counter to the sense of responsibility and makes of sin a subvolitional state of the soul, either inherited or acquired through some mysterious participation in the sin of Adam. The attempts that have been made in the past to harmonize a subvolitional conception of sin with personal responsibility, represent some of the most extraordinary intellectual contortions that have appeared in the history of Christian thought. And it is no mitigation of their fallacious and self-contradictory character that similar attempts are at present being made in influential theological circles.

Sin on a subconscious or subvolitional level is not sin in the proper sense of the term. It has no ethical or unethical quality. It is a hypothetical entity that serves as a kind of metaphysical basis for the feeling of absolute dependence and for the belief in man's moral helplessness. According to this conception of sin we are all sinners through and through, and hence of ourselves can do no good thing. But no such extreme doctrine is necessary as a theoretical basis for our Christian experience of dependence on God. This experience is emotional, it varies in degree, and even in its most absolute form is not inconsistent with a limited degree of independence on our part. We may feel an absolute dependence upon God without surrendering the consciousness of our own freedom. Feeling is one thing and a metaphysic a quite different thing. This has often been overlooked in theology. It is here that we have the basal error of historic Calvinism and of current Barthianism. They translate, or rather mistranslate, an emotional absolute into a metaphysical absolute.

Christian experience does not require belief in the absolute impotence and absolute sinfulness of man in order that its sense of dependence upon a Divine Power may be adequately grounded. Indeed, such a belief logically cancels freedom and responsibility and transforms a personal trustful dependence on God into fatalism. It thus undermines the consciousness of sin. Joseph Wood Krutch has said that "the modern man cannot sin." This is true, if the modern man is a determinist. Determinism, both naturalistic and theological, destroys the possibility of sin in the ethical sense of the term. And in any other sense the term is misleading and confusing. We gain nothing by extending sin into the subvolitional realm. We do not in this way deepen the sense of sin. We distort and disintegrate it. Sin to be real, to be a ground of self-condemnation, to be a condition of repentance, must have its root in human freedom. Subvolitional sin is not sin; and no attempt to deduce such a conception of sin from Christian experience is warranted either by conscience or reason.[8]

Our need of God grows out of our actual weakness and sinfulness, not out of theories with respect to them. To argue, as the strict Barthians do, that our weakness and sinfulness must be absolute, and that the recognition of any independent strength of our own leads to godless pride, is a piece of closet theologizing. It is not based on fact. On the contrary, it leads to self-contradiction and general befuddlement. If we are to think clearly on the subject of sin, we must distinguish between sin itself and the material of sin or what Paul calls "the passions of

[8] For a different view see Edwin Lewis, *The Christian Manifesto*, pp. 146ff.

sin." The passions of sin are not themselves sinful. They become such only when the will consents to their excessive and evil expression. It is also important to recognize that our need of moral redemption does not depend upon the traditional theory of original sin. It depends on the fact that as spiritual beings we have the task of moralizing the nonmoral impulses, desires, and interests with which we are endowed by birth, and that this task is enormously difficult, so difficult that it can be accomplished only through the transforming and redeeming power of the Divine Spirit. The need of redemption is thus factual, not theoretical. It is based on our own moral experience; and no other basis of the Christian doctrine of sin and redemption is necessary.[9]

The Divine Grace

Closely associated with the Christian consciousness of sin is the assurance of the divine grace. The two go together. Sin is the presupposition of the divine grace, and the divine grace is the sole means of escape from the bondage of sin. If we hold an extreme view of one, we must, to be logical, hold an extreme view of the other.

[9] For a more extended discussion of the topic dealt with in this section see my *Doctrine of Redemption,* pp. 151-168, 222-270.

If sin is absolute, so is the divine grace. If sin excludes the power of contrary choice in man, so does the divine grace. The two involve each other, and a change in our conception of the one carries with it a change in our conception of the other. Logically the doctrine of sin comes first. It is because we are by nature sinful and incapable of any good thing that we reject the synergistic view of the divine grace and look upon grace as unconditional, as wholly independent of any human initiative. But psychologically or empirically it is the absoluteness of the divine grace that comes first. We experience the greatness and goodness of God, and they so overwhelm us that they cast over our souls the deep shadow of impotence and sinfulness. We do not first feel our own sinfulness and nothingness, and then infer the greatness of the divine grace. It is not because we consider ourselves utterly helpless that we look upon God as great and good. It is because he seems to us transcendently great and gracious that we feel our helplessness. Our sense of unworthiness is a reflection of his holiness and love. His grace first manifests itself to us, and then we in the light of his infinite mercy disclaim any merit for ourselves and abase ourselves before him.

Such is the origin of all that the creeds say about original sin, the total depravity of man, and human impotence. These doctrines express our personal or emotional reaction to the sovereignty and grace of God; and when thus interpreted psychologically, they are intelligible and valid. They describe the normal human attitude toward Deity. But when interpreted metaphysically, they read into Christian experience a foreign and illusory element. Original sin and complete human impotence are not presuppositions or implications of Christian experience. To make them such is to transform an emotion into a metaphysic, and to construe Christian experience in terms of an obsolete and inconsistent philosophy. All that the experience of the divine grace requires is a profound sense of need, both moral and natural, and a consciousness of dependence on a Higher Power. A limited degree of freedom on man's part is not excluded; it is rather presupposed.[10] Clear insight into this truth and the vitalizing of it in Christian preaching and teaching was one of the most characteristic elements in the Wesleyan movement and perhaps its chief contribution to Christian theology.

---

[10] Freedom and grace are both necessary for the religious man. "If he abandons the former, he becomes a mere puppet in the universe, and, as such, incapable of the religious attitude; if he abandons the latter, he declines from religion to moralism, and has denied his need for God." W. R. Matthews, *God in Christian Thought and Experience*, p. 26.

Hope

Another fundamental and significant aspect of Christian experience is hope, which stands closely related to the experience of the divine grace. From the Christian standpoint man's only hope is in God. We ourselves have a measure of freedom; but this freedom offers no ground for self-sufficiency or pride. It is itself the gift of God, and its proper exercise is dependent on the divine grace. There is, therefore, no basis for self-righteousness. We do not and cannot save ourselves. We are saved, if at all, by faith in the divine goodness. The grace of God is the one source of our hope.

But hope takes various forms. There is, first, the hope of ultimate redemption, redemption from sin and death. This is the Christian hope in its deepest and most distinctive form. Here we stand face to face with the eternal, with the final issues of life. We are confronted with the last things, with the end of life; and despite all appearances to the contrary we affirm that the end is not what it seems to be; it is the beginning of life eternal. So utterly at variance with our common experience is this affirmation that more or less skepticism with reference to it is inevitable. At present there is considerably less stress on the life to come than there was in the past, and in some quarters the tendency is to treat it as though it belonged to the periphery of religion and was not an essential article of belief. But this tendency runs counter to the true genius of the Christian faith and is itself a sign of religious decay. Profound faith cannot be content with this world; it hopes for another, and this hope it bases on "the power of God." God is a God of the living, not of the dead; and because he is such, he cannot and will not permit our present union with him to be sundered by death. This was the teaching of Jesus, and this is the abiding conviction of the Christian Church.

Christian hope, however, is not confined to the future life. We hope not only for redemption from death but also for a better life on earth. The latter hope we have already to some extent realized, in so far as we are Christians; and we look forward to a further realization of it. The divine grace, as we understand it, guarantees us an ever richer and fuller life. Through it we may as individuals be saved both *in* our sins and *from* our sins. There is here a double truth. Each aspect of it has played an important rôle in Christian experience. The Reformation theology laid special stress on the idea that we are saved *in* our sins or despite our sins. This emphasis has been revived by Karl Barth and his associates. The idea underlying it is that we are all by nature sinful. We are unable of ourselves to attain the moral ideal. In its presence we all stand condemned. Hence if we are to escape the sense of condemnation, if we are to attain inner peace, it can be only through the divine grace, which takes the will for the deed and accepts us despite our shortcomings. In other words, we are saved *in* our sins. It is the only way we can be saved.

Under certain conditions this is a wholesome and comforting doctrine. If a person is actuated by an intense moral earnestness and is in a state of distress because he is unable to realize the moral ideal, it is a liberating and healing word to be told that he is saved by faith, not by works. It is not what he actually does but, rather, what he seeks to do, that wins the divine favor. His moral failures do not, therefore, necessarily condemn him. They may be forgiven, and when forgiven, life takes on a new zest and joy. Sin can be overcome only to a very limited degree in this world, and hence there is redeeming power in the assurance that God saves us *in* our sins.

But while this type of teaching has religious value and has figured prominently in the history of Protestantism, there is danger in it. When emphasized in a one-sided way, it may have a deadening effect on the moral will, it may discourage high moral endeavor, it may lead Christian people to be content with the ordinary moral standards of the day. The result is religious formalism and indifference. That was what took place in England in the latter part of the seventeenth and the beginning of the eighteenth century. When John Wesley appeared upon the scene, he found things in a deplorable state both morally and religiously. Something, he felt, must be done to alter the situation. A change of emphasis was imperatively needed. So instead of stressing the idea of salvation *in* our sins he emphasized the doctrine of salvation *from* our sins. Salvation itself was with him as with his evangelical predecessors a divine affair. It was effected through faith, not through works. But faith with him was a human as well as a divine act, and the most important thing connected with it was its moral and spiritual consequences. Holiness of life he regarded as an essential element in Christian experience. Faith, he held, was an ethical conception. Whatever he may have said to the contrary—and he often expressed himself in traditional Protestant terms—his real conviction was that faith is a free and at bottom a moral act. It is implicit regeneration. With him there was no justification without regeneration. A transformed life was involved in Christian experience, and the profounder the Christian experience, the more complete was the emancipation from sin. The process of emancipation, according to Wesley, was not necessarily held in check by the power of original sin. It might go on and ought to go on until the power of original sin was itself broken and the soul was restored "to its primitive health." A completely integrated moral life—what Wesley called perfect love or sanctification—was possible in this life, if men would only diligently seek it. This high note of moral optimism runs through his entire ministry.

No doubt there were inconsistencies, crudities, and excesses associated with his doctrine of Christian perfection. But this at least may be said to its credit that it is perhaps the most significant attempt ever made in the history of Christian thought to thoroughly moralize the conception of faith. Faith here ceases to be a magical substitute for good works, it ceases to be linked with a soul-enslaving fatalism and emerges as perfect love, triumphant over the sub-ethical limitations that traditional theology had imposed upon it. Whether such a completely moralized faith should be directly sought as a conscious experience may be a question. But this at least may be said that the intimate connection which Wesley established between faith and perfect love or sanctification is one of the profoundest and most significant developments in the history of Protestant theology. Holy living is not a mere adjunct to faith; it is vital faith itself, and as such possible of attainment here and now.

Since the time of Wesley the moral optimism of the Christian faith has been extended from the individual to society, and in this broader social application is at present receiving an extraordinary degree of attention. Some are denying the validity of this new development in Christian teaching. They are taking essentially the same attitude toward society that some Calvinists two centuries ago took toward the individual. As it was then said that the individual could not hope to escape from his sinful state in this life, so it is now being said that society is necessarily "immoral." There are demonic forces in it that we have no valid ground for believing will ever be exorcised. We may restrict to some extent their activity, and may to some extent improve economic and social conditions, but no real conversion of society, no radical transformation of its structure, is possible. Despite all our efforts society will continue to be essentially what it now is. There is, properly speaking, no social gospel. The basal mood of the Christian faith as over against both society and nature is *Aner-*

kennung, submission, acknowledgment of the sovereign will of God.[11]

On the other hand, there are those who practically identify the Gospel with social reform and to whom Christianity means primarily pacifism, socialism, prohibition, or some other modification of the existing social order. These people do not as a rule reject the historic message of the Church; but it has to a large degree lost its meaning for them. The Christian hope has become with them almost wholly a social hope. More or less radical economic and political theories have taken the place of the Christian doctrines of the past. A transformed society rather than transformed individuals has become their chief object of concern.

Both of these extreme positions have at present able representatives in the Church; but neither, we may be confident, will ever gain the ascendancy. The complete socializing or naturalizing of the Christian hope would be the end of Christianity. On the other hand, indifference to the social aspirations of the masses would be a betrayal of the Christian principle of love. It would isolate the Church from the onmoving current of the world's thought and life and reduce it to comparative impotence. The present

---

[11] Karl Barth, *The Doctrine of the Word of God,* pp. 233-238.

social and economic order is no longer regarded as an external fatality or as divinely decreed. It is obviously plastic, subject to change, and only by contributing to this change and giving proper direction to it can the Church adequately fulfill its ministry of good will in the world. This is coming to be more and more widely recognized. The only point that today divides the great body of Christian believers has to do with the best method of promoting social progress. The hope of such progress is at present inherent in normal Christian experience.[12]

God in Christ

The most distinctive element in Christian experience has to do with the experient's relation to the Person of Christ. This relation is not merely historical. It does not consist simply in the knowledge that Jesus was the founder of the Christian faith. It does not consist merely in the belief that he was the perfect exemplar of religious experience. It does not consist in the conviction that he was the one authoritative revealer of the true God. It is something more intimate than all this. It is a direct personal relation to a living Christ. It is a sense of his abiding presence. It is such an experience as Paul had when he said, "For me to live is Christ,"

[12] See H. F. Rall, *A Faith for Today*, pp. 261-278.

"I am crucified with Christ: nevertheless I live; yet not I, but Christ liveth in me."[13] This consciousness of mystical union with Christ varies in clearness and definiteness with different people. But to some degree it is implicit in all distinctively Christian experience. It is involved in the sense of the Divine Presence. God comes to us as the God and Father of our Lord Jesus Christ. Christ and Deity are for us indissolubly linked together. We cannot as Christians think one without thinking the other. God is for us a Christlike God. Our profoundest thought of Christ is that God was in him reconciling the world unto himself.[14] The thought of Christ thus carries with it the thought of God, and the thought of God carries with it the thought of Christ. It is so also in our Christian experience. To experience Christ is to experience God and to experience God is to experience Christ.[15]

There is, to be sure, a certain difference of connotation between the words "Christ" and

---

[13] Philippians 1. 21; Galatians 2. 20.

[14] 2 Corinthians 5. 19.

[15] In view of this fact it is doubtful if the distinction between "evangelical" and "mystical" has a place within Christian experience. Every truly Christian experience is an experience of Christ, and every experience of Christ is both an "evangelical" and a "mystical" experience. This was obviously true of Wesley's Aldersgate Street experience. To limit the word "evangelical" to the older type of conversion experience hardly seems warranted. See Umphrey Lee, *John Wesley and Modern Religion,* pp. 89ff.

"God." When we speak of "Christ" in the full religious sense of the term, we think of God from the standpoint of the incarnation; and when we speak of "God," we think of him from the standpoint of the universe as a whole. But the one involves the other, and it is a mistake to seek an experience of Christ distinct from that of God. The so-called Christ-mysticism of Paul is not essentially different from Christian mysticism in general. Both have to do with a direct experience of God and a direct experience of God in Christ.

That God was in Christ reconciling the world unto himself is a fundamental affirmation of the Christian faith and a presupposition of Christian experience. Christian experience would lose its distinctive character, if less than this were affirmed with reference to Christ. But how to conceive of the presence of God in Christ, is one of the most perplexing questions that has engaged the attention of Christian thinkers. Many different solutions of the problem have been proposed. Some have been labeled orthodox and some heterodox. I have my own solution, a theory which I have elaborated elsewhere and which I should like to think of as combining the truth of both orthodoxy and heterodoxy.[16] But

[16] *The Doctrine of Redemption*, pp. 273-333.

no theory, whatever value it may have, is essential to Christian experience.

All Christological theories, in so far as they are self-consistent, are based on some particular type of philosophy; and in this respect they serve an apologetic purpose. They offer a more or less rational justification of the Christian view of Christ. But none of them are necessary deductions from the data of Christian experience. All that Christian experience affirms is that God was in Christ and that he was in him for the purpose of reconciling the world unto himself. It says nothing about the mode of the divine immanence or the method of the reconciliation. These are problems left to human speculation. All that Christian experience is concerned with is the fact of Christ, the fact of his unique relation to God, the fact of his reconciling activity. If God was actually in him reconciling the world unto himself, we need nothing more. That is sufficient ground for assigning to him the position of divine leadership which he has occupied in Christian experience from the beginning.

It has been argued that the basis of Jesus' authority is to be found in his sinlessness.[17] Religious error, we are told, is due to man's native tendency to "rationalize"; and "rationalization"

---

[17] Cyril H. Valentine, *Modern Psychology and the Validity of Christian Experience,* pp. XVII, 11f., 22f., 33, 45.

has its origin in repressions, complexes, conflicts, obsessions, and other inward disorders. These disorders had no place in Jesus' life. He was sinless, and hence "free from all inner causes of rationalizing." There is, therefore, no reason why his religious experience should not be regarded as "infallible" and his teaching as trustworthy. His sinless nature "guarantees the truthfulness of the revelation" received through him.

In this argument it is assumed, and rightly, that the unperverted religious nature of man may be accepted as an authentic revelation of objective reality. Jesus represented human nature in its "most highly developed" form and, consequently, his witness to the existence and nature of God may properly be regarded as our "most trustworthy authority" on the subject. But while this line of argument is in principle valid, there are two reservations that need to be made. One is that the religious nature of man is active, not passive. It was so with Jesus. His "sinlessness" was a spiritual achievement, not a metaphysical inheritance. His perfect religious experience was a product of creative energy, not a passive reflection of an objective order. When we, then, speak of his revelation of God, we must do so in terms of creativity, not of mere receptivity.

The other reservation has to do, not with the nature of Jesus' sinlessness, but with its historicity. The argument under consideration assumes that Jesus lived a sinless life; but no proof is offered, and no proof is possible. The question consequently arises as to whether such an assumption can legitimately be used as evidence of the truth of Jesus' teaching. Most people would probably admit that if Jesus actually lived an absolutely sinless life, his teaching would be entitled to a greater degree of credence than would otherwise be the case. But they would probably also confess that they find it easier to believe in the validity of his teaching than in his absolute sinlessness. The latter is a more difficult article of faith than the former. In any case it logically comes second, not first. We do not infer the credibility of Jesus' world view from his sinlessness, but, rather, the reverse. It is the impression of trustworthiness made upon us by his total life and teaching that leads us later to infer his sinlessness. The only apologetic value that his sinlessness has is that it removes from his inner life certain psychological obstacles to the attainment of truth with which *we* have to contend. Logically it makes no contribution to the solution of our problem. It is, rather, a part of the problem itself.

A distinguished German scholar has said that

it was not Jesus who conquered the ancient world, but a myth about him. A more correct statement would be that it was the religious interpretation of Jesus' personality, not what we might call the visible Personality itself, that effected the triumph of Christianity. From almost the beginning it was realized that in Jesus' life and work there was operative not only a human quest after God but a divine quest after man. Of the two the latter was far the more important. It was the divine quest after man, the God in Christ, that constituted the organizing center of the Christian faith and that through the centuries has given to Christian experience its most distinctive trait. In the presence of Christ we feel ourselves face to face with One who is more than a prophet, more than an example, more than a symbol; we feel ourselves face to face with the Son, the express image of the Father. It is this fact, the instinctive response of the Christian heart and mind to the divine in Christ, that gives to him his place in Christian prayer and worship.[18]

Of the four fundamental aspects of Christian experience that we have considered, the first three—the consciousness of sin, the assurance of the divine grace, and hope both temporal and eternal—appear to some extent in all the higher

[18] See my *Doctrine of God,* pp. 390-394.

religions. But they are mediated to us through Christ, and through faith in him they become our personal possession. In their Christian form they consequently have a unique character. They are colored by the personality of Christ, and they also receive from him a distinctive emphasis.

The mediation of Christ is a fact of history and experience, not a metaphysical theory. It was not a commercial, legal, or governmental device, whereby the forgiveness of sin was made possible. The theories of the atonement, based on such assumptions, are to be regarded as metaphorical. They are figurative expressions of the divine grace manifest in Christ. The great fact is that God was in Christ in such a pre-eminent degree that in and through him we have come to know God. He has as a mere fact of history mediated to us the knowledge of God, and his name has, furthermore, become so closely associated with that of Deity that for us the experience of the Living Christ is the experience of God himself. This conviction is wrought into the very fabric of our Christian experience, and finds its justification in virtually the whole of Christian history.

Conclusion

In concluding our study of Christian experience it may be well to recall to mind some of the more important points in the preceding discussion.

For one thing, the divine grace is in a sense both the beginning and the end of our redemption. We instinctively acknowledge this truth in our prayers. God is the source of everything that is good within us. But in so expressing ourselves we need to distinguish between the language of emotion and devotion and the language of theology. If we take the language of prayer in strict literalness and make of it a metaphysical theory, we inevitably fall into a theology which denies human freedom, which affirms the inherent sinfulness of man, and which makes the ultimate fate of the individual dependent upon the arbitrary will of God—a doctrine that may not improperly be described as the worst moral scandal in the history of Christian thought. An emotional absolute is not a safe basis for a metaphysical theology. The heart does not make the theologian; it more frequently unmakes him. It was the translation or rather mistranslation of an emotion into a metaphysic that led to the Calvinistic doctrine of predestination, and that led also to the Catholic doctrine of the objective sanctity of the Church. These doctrines as expressions of emotional attitudes toward God and toward the Church may have their value. But as metaphysical theories they are altogether untenable. One destroys moral responsibility, and the other transforms holiness into an impersonal substance. If we are to have a sound theology, we must be guided by the head, not merely by the heart.

Another point that needs emphasis is the actual presence of God in human life and in the world, a presence conditioned by our own initiative. There is, it is true, danger of stressing our own initiative in a one-sided way. Along this line lies humanism. There is also danger in awakening the expectation of an unconditioned and lawless advent of the divine into human life. Along this line lies fanaticism. But between fanaticism and humanism there is a middle position which insists on the possibility of a free and ordered co-operation between the human and the divine and on the rich fruitage of such co-operation in the life of mankind, both individual and social. It is in this view that we have the basis of a comprehensive Christian optimism. An ultimate optimism, so far as the individual is concerned, has always been characteristic of Christianity. Eternal life has been the assured reward of the Christian believer. A present moral transformation of the individual has also been a promise of the Christian faith. But the extent of this possible transformation has been and still is a subject of dispute. At this point there have been both a pessimistic and an optimistic school of thought. The latter received an extraordinary stimulus through the work of the Wesleys, and at present probably represents the dominant tendency in Anglo-Saxon Protestantism.

Optimism, so far as the transformation of the present social order is concerned, is a recent development within the Church, and with reference to it there are still wide differences of opinion. Theologically there is no valid objection to it, and ethically it would seem to be a consequent of the Christian principle of love. But how far it is warranted by what Emil Brunner would call "the orders of creation,"[19] can be determined only by experience itself. All that we need insist upon is that such a social hope is congenial to the spirit and genius of the Christian faith and that it has a proper place in Christian experience. The Christian faith in God is also a faith in the possibilities of the world that he has made.

Of Christian experience it may, then, be said that its older dualistic framework is gone, but that its essential content remains unchanged. It is still faith in a living God and a living Christ;

[19] *Das Gebot und die Ordnungen,* pp. 275ff. English translation, entitled *The Divine Imperative,* pp. 291ff.